CLASSIC CHINESE LEGENDS

© Illustrations Evelyn Lip
© 1990 Times Editions Pte Ltd
Reprinted 1996

Published by Times Books International
an imprint of Times Editions Pte Ltd
Times Centre
1 New Industrial Road
Singapore 536196

Times Subang
Lot 46, Subang Hi-Tech Industrial Park
Batu Tiga
40000 Shah Alam
Selangor Darul Ehsan
Malaysia

Set in Galliard 11 points over 14 points

Printed in Singapore

ISBN 981 204 208 3

CLASSIC CHINESE LEGENDS

Evelyn Lip

TIMES BOOKS INTERNATIONAL
Singapore • Kuala Lumpur

Preface

The Chinese have a long and rich history spanning 5000 years. They draw their cultural traditions, beliefs and ceremonies from this past, including a rich store of myths and legends which was at first handed down by word of mouth and later written as novels.

Chinese mythology is peopled with gods, goddesses, fairies and spirits who are not paragons of virtue, but rather much like human beings with the same follies and foibles. Thus, there are mischievous sun gods who scorch the earth (*The Ten Suns*) and playful and quarrelsome immortals who fight among themselves over trivials (*Eight Immortals Crossing the Sea*).

On the other hand, historical heroes become legendary figures as history and myth merge. Men and women of courage and virtue (among them monks, statesmen, warriors, poets, philosophers and patriots) became larger than life as stories of their exploits were retold through the ages.

This collection of myths and legends reflects the rich cultural fabric of the Chinese. Some of the legends are based on real-life heroes whose exploits caught the imagination of the people. Many are social comments of the period in which they are set. All serve to reinforce traditions, values, the cultural and social structures of the Chinese.

Evelyn Lip
1990

Contents

Journey to the West

Journey to the West, *or Xi You Ji, is a novel written in the sixteenth century by Wu Cheng En, a Ming dynasty scholar. Told and retold countless times over the centuries, it is still very popular for it portrays the follies and foibles of man through a fantastic journey full of adventure and cliffhanging situations. It relates the hardships of Tang dynasty Buddhist monk Tang San Zhuang, who went west in search of Buddhist scriptures, and describes how he met and obtained help from Sun Wu Kong the monkey king, Zhu Bajie the boar spirit, and Sha Seng the sand spirit.*

The author of Journey to the West *made use of characters in the fascinating story to reflect his own frustration of being an unrecognized scholar under the oppressive Ming ruling class. His disappointments and his frustration over the political situation can be detected in the beginning of the book in which Sun Wu Kong created havoc in the western paradise, an episode from the novel retold here. The story that follows this relates the encounter with the White Bone Demon.*

Sun Wu Kong Creates Havoc in the Western Paradise

The king of monkeys lived on the Mountain of Flowers and Fruits, Hua Guo Shan. It was said that he was born from an ancient rock. He was highly skilled in *wushu** and had supernatural powers. He could change himself into any of seventy-two forms of being and he could traverse long distances in the blink of an eye. Equipped with such powers he was quite fearless.

One day the monkey king decided that he should have a weapon of the quality that was worthy of his status and his powers. So he travelled far and wide in search of such a weapon, but he could not find anything suitable. As there was nothing suitable on land, he decided to look in the sea instead. When he reached the sea, he dived into the icy-cold water, descending many leagues until he reached the bottom of the sea.

There he saw a huge palace of crystal guarded by all manner of sea creatures. He swam towards the palace but was stopped at the gate by a soldier with the head of a prawn and the body of a man. With the mere stroke of his finger, the monkey king threw the soldier a few metres away. Then, before the other guards could take him on, he kicked at the gate which fell with a crash. The guards were shocked and too afraid to engage him in a fight. Instead they swam as fast as they could to report the matter to the dragon king.

The monkey king presented himself before the dragon king and brazenly said that he expected to be given the best weapon in the kingdom of the sea. Angered, the dragon king fought the monkey king, but was no match for the latter. So he presented the monkey king with the most valuable thing in his kingdom, the *ding hai zhen*, the needle which stabilizes the sea.

* *wushu* – Chinese martial arts

The triumphant monkey king lifted the thirteen thousand pound needle as if it were a mere wooden stick. After he had swung the weapon around him with great skill, he blew a breath on it, changing it into a tiny needle which he immediately tucked in his right ear, much to the amazement of all present.

The news that the monkey king had taken the *ding hai zhen* reached the ears of the Jade Emperor of the heavens and he summoned the mischievous primate to the Jade Palace. Knowing that punishing the cocky and insubordinate monkey king would only lead to further revolt and havoc, the Jade Emperor offered him a job in the heavens so that he could keep an eye on him.

'From this day on you shall be called Qi Tian Da Sheng, saint of the entire heavenly paradise,' the Jade Emperor pronounced.

'I thank Your Majesty,' the monkey king said graciously, feeling quite pleased with himself.

But the monkey king's happiness was short-lived. He soon found out that his job was only looking after horses in the heavenly paradise. He was left out of most activities in paradise. When he found out that he was not invited to the birthday party of the goddess of the western paradise, Xi Wang Mu, it was the last straw. He decided to gate crash.

Upon arrival at the garden of the western paradise, he found that the place was bustling with activity as fairies hurried about with the preparation for the important occasion. Filled with resentment at being totally ignored, the monkey king cast a spell on the busy fairies who froze in mid-action. He went about taunting them as they could not retaliate. Then he poured the good wine down his throat and ate as many peaches of longevity as he could, all the while proclaiming that he was the only worthy guest at the party. Finally he swallowed the pill of immortality prepared by the immortal Daoist Tai Shang Lao Jun. Laughing and swaying like a drunk, the monkey king put some peaches and food in a big bag. Then with a somersault he was back in Hua Guo Shan, his home.

Upon hearing the havoc wreaked by the contemptuous monkey king, the Jade Emperor was furious. He summoned a host of warriors to arrest the mischief maker.

When the warriors arrived at the beautiful Hua Guo Shan, they confronted the monkey king, who proved elusive and difficult to capture. However, fighting alone, he was no match for the warriors and was finally captured and brought back to the Jade Palace where he was tortured and thrown into a furnace. But the monkey king emerged from the furnace unharmed and smiling, for he had eaten the immortality pill and was now an immortal. The perplexed warriors went to the Jade Emperor who decided to enlist the help of the Buddha.

The monkey king was brought before the Buddha who stretched out his hand and challenged the monkey king to stand for a moment on his palm. Without hesitation the monkey king did so, reducing himself to the size of the Buddha's palm. Immediately the Buddha turned his palm over, trapping the monkey king, who was eventually imprisoned in a hill resembling the Buddha's palm. This hill, known as Wu Zi Shan, was sealed with a *fu* (spell), a yellow piece of cloth with magic words written by the Buddha, which could only be broken by a Buddhist monk Tang San Zhuang. This monk would only do so if the monkey king promised to accompany him on his journey to the west.

For many years, the monkey king lived a life of solitary confinement, reflecting on the blissful life he once led on Hua Guo Shan and longing for the freedom he had lost.

For years, the monkey king waited for someone to rescue him. But no one even went near enough to talk to him. Night and day were the same to him. Life was like death. Then one day he heard footsteps outside his cell.

'Help! Help! Please help me out of here!' he shouted.

'So you are the mischievous one. You have to promise me to behave before I let you out,' the voice outside said.

'Yes, yes, I promise. I promise to accompany you to the west if you peel off the *fu* and let me out of here,' the monkey king said quickly, believing that his interlocutor was the monk the Buddha spoke about.

Outside, Tang San Zhuang the monk, who felt sorry for the monkey king, decided to peel off the *fu*. Immediately the hill exploded with a thunderous boom, hurling masses of rocks into all directions. The monkey king jumped out of his prison, laughing uncontrollably and jumping up and down.

'Thank you, thank you for releasing me. I have been imprisoned for so long I really deserve a long holiday and hundreds of good meals. Good bye!'

'Wait, I have a present for you,' the Buddhist monk said as he handed a golden crown to the overjoyed monkey king.

'Thank you. This is beautiful,' the monkey king exclaimed as he put the crown on.

'You have promised to help on my journey to the west. Are you coming with me now?' asked the Buddhist monk.

'Sorry, I have too many things to do. Maybe I will see you again some time,' the monkey king said as he bade farewell.

Tang San Zhuang did not try to stop the monkey king but closed his eyes and started to pray, whereupon the monkey king began to reel in pain.

'Oh, oh! It is unbearable, please stop saying your prayer,' the monkey king entreated. Tang San Zhuang stopped saying his prayer and the pain stopped immediately.

'It must be the crown you gave me that is causing the pain. I'm returning it to you,' the monkey king said and tried to remove the crown.

But, try as he might, he could not remove it. Again and again he tried to escape but the monk would start to pray each time and the pain would return. The monkey king realized that he had no choice but to keep his promise and help the monk on his journey in quest of Buddhist scriptures. Tang San Zhuang gave him the name Sun Wu Kong meaning One Who Realizes that at the End One Possesses Nothing.

Tang San Zhuang and the White Bone Demon

Not long after they set out on their journey, Tang San Zhuang and Sun Wu Kong met Zhu Bajie the boar spirit and Sha Seng the sand spirit, who also became the Buddhist monk's disciples. Their first dangerous encounter with evil spirits was with the White Bone Demon.

It was a windy day and Tang San Zhuang and his disciples had reached the top of a hill after a long, tiring walk. They decided to take a rest and Sun Wu Kong, the ablest of the disciples, volunteered to look for food and water. Before he left he drew a magic ring with his golden staff encircling his companions so that no one could harm them. Behind a huge pine tree nearby, the White Bone Demon could not suppress a huge grin. This was her opportunity to capture Tang San Zhuang whose flesh she heard could make her immortal.

Tang San Zhuang felt a sudden rush of wind blowing towards him, dispelling the desolate stillness and sending hundreds of fallen leaves dancing in the air. Little did he know that this was caused by the crafty White Bone Demon. Then, out of nowhere, a pretty young maiden carrying a basket of food appeared before the monk and his two disciples. She tried to go near them but she could not as she was repelled by the magic ring. So she took the cover off her food basket, revealing the steaming hot buns. The hungry Zhu Bajie could hardly resist the temptation to reach out for the fragrant buns but he dared not step out of the ring.

The young maiden, noticing his agitation, goaded him, 'Come and have a bun; they are very good.'

Unable to resist any longer, Zhu Bajie pulled his master with him out of the ring towards the maiden. The moment they stepped out of the ring, the young maiden grabbed hold of Tang San Zhuang. However, before she could make away with the monk, Sun Wu Kong jumped down from a moving cloud and struck the maiden with his magic staff. Immediately a swarm of bees attacked him. As he was fending off the bees, the White Bone Demon fled the body of the maiden.

'How can you repay kindness with such a wicked deed? The poor maiden was offering us food, and you killed her! I hear you were mischievous, but you are evil,' the disappointed Tang San Zhuang said.

'But Master, she was not a maiden but a demon,' Sun Wu Kong tried to explain.

'If she is a demon, she would not lie dead here before me.' So saying Tang San Zhuang turned his back on his recalcitrant disciple and walked away. The other two disciples quickly caught up with him. Sun Wu Kong followed at a distance, knowing that his master was displeased with him.

They had not gone too far when they met an old woman who eagerly offered them her basket of fruits and cooked food. With all her charm, she could not fool the monkey king who saw through her disguise and knew that she was the White Bone Demon. He decided not to take chances and struck the old woman with his staff. Tang San Zhuang, furious that the unrepentant disciple was bent on destruction, began to chant his prayers to punish him. Sun Wu Kong staggered in pain, incapacitated, and the White Bone Demon took the opportunity to escape.

When his master had stopped chanting and the pain had gone away, Sun Wu Kong tried to explain to him again why he had struck the old woman, but the monk refused to listen. Instead, he walked briskly on, the other disciples trailing behind.

15

Not long after, an old man walking with a limp approached Tang San Zhuang. Again, Sun Wu Kong could see that it was the White Bone Demon in disguise. So he leaped suddenly at the old man. But before he could strike, Tang San Zhuang began to chant his prayers and caused him so much pain that he had to let the demon go.

Tang San Zhuang was so disappointed in Sun Wu Kong that he ordered him to leave, saying,

'From now on you are no longer my disciple.'

No amount of pleading on the part of the monkey king could move the monk. There was nothing for it but to return to Hua Guo Shan.

Tang San Zhuang carried on his journey west with his two other disciples Zhu Bajie and Sha Seng. Late that evening, they came upon a dilapidated temple where they decided to rest for the night. On the altar full of cobwebs there was a row of deities. Tan San Zhuang knelt before the statues to pray. At that moment, a gust of smoke filled the hall, almost blinding, and choking all present. Through the veil of smoke, Tang San Zhuang and his disciples saw the icons coming to life, all taking the visage of bone demons, the middle one being white and bigger, uglier and more evil-looking than the rest. The White Bone Demon swooped down from the altar and gathered up the monk and, together with her followers, bore the monk to the White Bone Demon Cave.

Zhu Bajie and Sha Seng were no match for the White Bone Demon and her disciples. They could not do anything to stop their master's capture. So they raced as fast as they could to Hua Guo Shan to seek Sun Wu Kong's help.

At Hua Guo Shan, Sun Wu Kong was not at all disturbed. He sent his fellow disciples back, and, with a big somersault, arrived at the entrance of the White Bone Demon Cave. There, he turned himself into an insect and flew into the cave. He saw his master tied to a post near a cauldron of boiling water. The

孫悟空大戰白骨精

Sun Wu Kong fighting the White Bone Demon.

17

demons were taunting and teasing him.

Then Zhu Bajie and Sha Seng arrived at the Cave and demanded the release of their master. The demons refused and a fight ensued. Again the two were defeated and were tied up as well. The demons prepared to throw their victims into the cauldron. Before they could do so, however, Sun Wu Kong reverted to his original form and challenged the demons. He fought well and rescued his master and fellow disciples, destroying the White Bone Demon and her disciples in the process.

The four then continued on their journey west.

Madam White Snake

Madam White Snake is the heroine of a romantic legend popularized and written as early as the Southern Song period (A.D. 420–479). The story was elaborated further in the Ming dynasty by Chen Liu Long and renamed Lei Feng Ji. Later during the Qing period it was dramatized by Huang Tu Bi and Fang Cheng Pai and retitled Lei Feng Ta. It has been enacted in operas and period dramas countless times.

In the mountainous region of the remote province of Sichuan in the far west, there stood a mysterious cave of majestic height, veiled by mist and cloud throughout the year. This cave was Bai Yun Dong (White Cloud Cave) and it was on the mighty Er Mei Shan (Mount Er Mei). In the cave lived a white snake spirit who had acquired supernatural and *wushu* skills after a thousand years of training and abstaining from evil thoughts and deeds. As a result of her meditation and training she had become a jing, or spirit. She called herself Bai Su Zhen.

One day Bai Su Zhen met another snake spirit who had trained for five hundred years. This younger snake was named Xiao Qing because she was a green snake. The two snake spirits had a duel and it was not surprising that Bai Su Zhen won as she had trained for a much longer period. Xiao Qing admired Bai Su Zhen who in turn respected the former. Thus, they became close friends and sworn sisters.

The snake spirits, although they had no want for anything, often felt lonely in the vast emptiness in which nothing was visible except the tops of the hills and the shadowed valleys. Very often they sat under the majestic pine trees and gazed at the hardly visible red and green roofs of houses in the shadowed valleys below their paradise.

One full moon night, the sworn sisters were again talking wistfully of the peopled earth below when on an impulse they decided to leave their home on Er Mei Shan and venture into the busy human world of Hangzhou. They used their *wushu* skills and within a short time they arrived at Hangzhou where they were entranced by the beauty of the place, the hustle and bustle of city life and the fragrance of cooked food. They were excited, mesmerized by everything they saw, which was beyond their wildest expectation.

One day, a week after they arrived in Hangzhou, Bai Su Zhen and Xiao Qing were again out in the city centre. Amidst the earthly people they mingled with, one man stood out, being endowed with good looks and charm. Bai Su Zhen was impressed by him and decided to follow him as he walked towards the lake. Suddenly the sky was overcast with threatening black clouds and before long rain poured down from the sky. By the rickety jetty of the large lake was a small boat with a thatched roof, rocking like a cradle.

The young man ran swiftly onto the boat out of the rain. He was followed by Bai Su Zhen and Xiao Qing who had the same idea of travelling home in the covered boat. The boat owner asked the two women to leave because the young man was the first to reach the boat and so was the customer he should serve. Fortunately the young man spoke to the boat owner and asked him to allow the two maidens to stay as his guests. Bai Su Zhen came forward and thanked the young man who introduced himself as Xu Xian. Thus, a conversation was struck and Bai Su Zhen soon learnt that Xu Xian was an honest and trustworthy man. At the end of the boat trip Bai Su Zhen invited Xu Xian to visit her at her house.

Bai Su Zhen and Xu Xian were very much in love and, not long after they met, they were married in a simple ceremony. Together, with the help of Xiao Qing, they ran a shop selling medicinal herbs. They named the shop Bao He Tang (Hall of Protection and Harmony), quite appropriately. Bai Su Zhen and Xu Xian worked very diligently and earned the trust and respect of their clients. Their business was very successful. This aroused the jealousy of the chief monk of Jin Shan Temple, Fa Hai, who also had a shop selling herbs to the sick.

His ire prompted Fa Hai to find out more about the owners of Bao He Tang. Before long, he stumbled upon the secret of Bai Su Zhen. One day in his yellow monk's robe and holding a staff in his hand, he came to Bao He Tang.

'I have come to request donations and alms from your master,' said Fa Hai to the shop assistant.

Xu Xian, who saw him from behind his counter, took a few coins from his pocket and respectfully handed them to the monk. But Fa Hai caught hold of Xu Xian and exclaimed,

'Young man, you are possessed by an evil spirit. You will soon die if you don't do something.'

'How can you be sure! I am feeling fine. Who is this evil being?' asked Xu Xian in disbelief.

'Benefactor, I am afraid I have to be frank with you in order to save your life. Your wife is a snake spirit and she will consume your earthly life in no time,' warned Fa Hai, a frown creasing his forehead.

'How can you accuse my beloved wife of being a demon? I don't believe you!' remonstrated an enraged Xu Xian.

'Look, why should I lie to you? To prove what I have said

is true you have to do as I tell you. If I have lied you will know so,' promised Fa Hai. He then gave Xu Xian a bottle of special wine called *hong huang* and instructed him to let his wife drink it on the fifth day of the fifth lunar month. He also told him to pour sulphur powder around the perimeter of the house on the morning of the fifth moon festival.

'Follow my instructions faithfully and you'll see your wife reverting back to her original self,' Fa Hai said, his eyebrows raised and his eyes half closed.

The fifth day of the fifth lunar month arrived with Xu Xian waking from a terrible nightmare. Bai Su Zhen had got out of bed earlier in the morning and she did not notice her husband perspiring and gasping for breath when he awoke. Xu Xian tried to avoid seeing and talking to his wife because he felt a sense of uneasiness and guilt. But Bai Su Zhen was too busy with her housework and preparing a feast for her shop assistants and her family for the celebration of the festival to notice his strange behaviour.

The shop assistants were in a festive mood and they had brought along some *hong huang* wine which produced a strong smell that repelled Xiao Qing and Bai Su Zhen. But Bai Su Zhen was not terribly worried because she had a thousand years of training. So long as she did not drink it she knew she would be all right. But Xiao Qing was concerned that she would be affected so she made an excuse and went to bed early.

Bai Su Zhen served her shop assistants with food and cakes and then sat down to dine with Xu Xian who waited for the right moment to bring out his bottle of *hong huang* wine. Bai Su Zhen was unnerved by the sight and the smell of the wine. She tried to turn away but Xu Xian caught hold of her left hand and made her sit still while he poured the wine into a large cup.

'Come, my love, I offer you this drink which symbolizes my love for you. You must drink it to show you accept my love,' said Xu, fighting the fear and anxiety that rose to his throat.

Bai Su Zhen wanted to refuse his offer but was afraid that her husband's feelings might be hurt. She decided to take the risk, quite confident that she could withstand the effect of the strong wine. Xu Xian pressed on with his request and brought the cup of wine to her quivering lips. Bai Su Zhen drank the wine in a single gulp. Within seconds she felt the ceiling of the room whirling, her head spinning and her ears burning. She hastily excused herself and ran inside her bedroom and into bed. Gasping for breath and groaning with pain, she lost consciousness.

Xu Xian realized that something was wrong but told himself that his wife was not used to drinking and was just a little drunk. He walked towards the bed and peeped through the drawn curtains embroidered with mandarin ducks which reminded him of the love shared by him and his wife. His heart pounded with uneven rhythm as, his hands shaking, he pushed aside first the curtain and then the blanket that covered his wife. To his utter shock and horror he saw a huge, long and shimmering white snake lying motionless on the bed. His body trembled violently, then his heart stopped beating as he fell to the ground.

Xiao Qing woke up suddenly from her dream with a sense of dread that something terrible had happened. She rushed into Bai Su Zhen's bedroom and found Xu Xian motionless on the floor, with no pulse. She gave a sharp cry and woke her sister who had by now regained her human form as the effects of the wine had worn off. Bai Su Zhen was completely taken by grief and sorrow.

'Crying and moaning will not bring back honourable brother-in-law's life,' Xiao Qing admonished, and urged Bai Su Zhen to think of ways of saving Xu Xian. Putting aside her sorrow, Bai Su Zhen racked her brain. She remembered that on Kun Lun Shan there grew a grass of life called *ling zi cao* which could bring a person back to life if the body had not lost

Xu Xian discovers to his horror that Bai Su Zhen has turned into a white snake.

its warmth.

'No matter how high the hill or how difficult the path I will get the *ling zi cao* back before my husband's body turns cold,' Bai Su Zhen vowed with much determination.

After placing Xu Xian's body on a warm *kang**, Bai Su Zhen raced through thousands of hills and crossed many perilous seas. She travelled without rest to the mighty Kun Lun Shan.

Finally she reached the crest of the hills where sweet scents from strange flowers and plants filled the air and dense mist shrouded the rugged sides. Amidst the most extraordinarily coloured plants and the most awkwardly shaped rocks was the elixir of life, the *ling zi cao*, shining with a brilliance seldom seen. Bai Su Zhen leapt towards it and plucked it up. But her happiness was short-lived because the miraculous plant was snatched from her fingers by two guardians of the fairy garden. These guardians had magical powers and they soon overpowered Bai Su Zhen. They wanted to punish her for stealing the elixir of life but they were stopped by the old immortal Nan Ji Xian Weng who appeared as the guardians were poised to strike. He insisted that Bai Su Zhen be given a chance to explain herself. Bai Su Zhen knelt down and with tears in her eyes related her story to the immortal and the guardians of the garden. Touched by her steadfast love, they let her go with the magical *ling zi cao*.

Bai Su Zhen raced back, faster than her outward journey, her heart filled with hope. When she returned home Xu Xian's body was still warm. She boiled the *ling zi cao* with water and forced the boiled elixir down her husband's throat. Miraculously he recovered, complaining that he had had a nightmare. He vaguely remembered seeing a snake in bed, and the memory of Fa Hai and his warning rippled in his mind. He became suspicious of his wife's true identity. But Bai Su Zhen was even

---

* *kang* – a brick bed warmed by a fire under it.

more devoted to him than before, and he slowly forgot the past.

Time flew by quickly. Soon it was time to celebrate the fifth moon festival again. On the day of the festival, Fa Hai, the chief monk, again appeared at Bao He Tang. He tried to convince Xu Xian that his wife had indeed turned into a white snake the year before and that if he did not leave her he would be doomed. Xu Xian, appalled by the thought that he would be consumed by a snake demon, went back with Fa Hai to the Jin Shan Temple. Fa Hai, having lured Xu Xian to the temple, locked him up in the dungeon.

Bai Su Zhen waited for Xu Xian to return but in vain. She was terribly worried about his safety having heard that he had left with a strange looking monk and sent Xiao Qing out to look for him. When she learnt that Xu Xian was imprisoned by Fa Hai, she was determined to rescue him. Bai Su Zhen and Xiao Qing went as fast as they could to Jin Shan Temple. When they came to the violent sea that separated them from the temple, which was on a rocky island, Bai Su Zhen threw one of her shoes into the dark, roaring water and it turned into a boat. Bai Su Zhen and Xiao Qing jumped onto the rocking boat and rowed as hard as they could across the surging sea. As they neared the island, they could see the dark pine trees and treacherous rocks, like so many sharp daggers poised to kill. The steep cliffs made the island almost impregnable. The booming surf sounded intimidating but they rowed on with all their might. At last they reached the shore of Jin Shan where Fa Hai stood waiting. Swallowing her pride she knelt before Fa Hai and begged him to let her husband return home with her. But Fa Hai refused and ordered her to leave.

The following day, Bai Su Zhen and Xiao Qing returned and pleaded again with Fa Hai to let Xu Xian go. Again, Fa Hai refused. Bai Su Zhen knew then that she had no choice but to use force; she turned to the four dragon kings for help.

The four dragon kings caused the waters to change into huge waves that roared and howled. A terrific hurricane flooded Jin Shan. The villagers on the island were terrified. Using his magic robe, Fa Hai deterred the encroachment of the floods. Then, with the help of some minor gods, he overpowered Bai Su Zhen. Xiao Qing came in the nick of time to rescue her, and, together, they broke into Xu Xian's cell and bore him away.

Thus, Xu Xian and Bai Su Zhen were reunited. Not long after, a boy was born to them, on the fifteenth day of the twelfth lunar month. They called the boy Meng Jiao.

When Meng Jiao was one month old Fa Hai appeared and once again overpowered Bai Su Zhen, with his magic bowl. Bai Su Zhen knew that she was destined to be punished because many lives were lost during the deluge of Jin Shan. She realized that neither the four dragon kings nor other sympathetic gods could come to her rescue. Bai Su Zhen was imprisoned in a pagoda by the side of the West Lake in Hangzhou. Only the filial piety of her son could release her from her incarceration.

Not long after the capture of Bai Su Zhen, Xu Xian died of grief. Meng Jiao was left in the care of Bai Su Zhen's sworn sister, Xiao Qing. He grew up an intelligent and industrious boy. In time, he took the imperial examinations which he passed with top honours. But he could not forget the story his aunt Xiao Qing told him, about his mother.

After Meng Jiao had received his award from the emperor he went to the pagoda where his mother was imprisoned and prayed for her release. Thunder roared and lightning struck, and the pagoda burst open, releasing Bai Su Zhen who ran into her son's embrace. Then, just as suddenly, the wind died down, the sky stopped flashing and all was peace again.

The eight immortals – Lan Cai He, Cao Guo Jiu, Zhong Li Quan, Lu Dong Bin, Zhang Guo Lao, He Xian Gu, Han Xiang Zi and Li Tie Guai.

Eight Immortals Crossing the Sea

First written during the Tang dynasty, the adventures of the eight immortals are popular even to this day. Originally human beings, they became immortals after years of meditation and abstaining from evil thoughts and deeds. Some had eaten the peach of immortality and so had gained supernatural powers and immortality.

Lan Cai He was patron·of florists and carried a basket of flowers while Cao Guo Jiu was brother of the Empress Cao of the Song dynasty, and wore an embroidered robe and carried a pair of castanets. Zhong Li Quan, a fat man and warrior, held a magic fan; Lu Dong Bin the scholar held a sword. The elderly Zhang Guo Lao had a magic wood drum as weapon while He Xian Gu, the only female in the group, held a lotus. Han Xiang Zi, still revered as the patron of musicians, had a magic flute. Li Tie Guai, the cripple, had a crutch in one hand and a magic gourd in the other. Together they lived on the Isles of the Blessed in the Eastern Sea.

It was the birthday of the goddess of the western paradise. In the garden of paradise, the sun splashed its glorious rays over the splendid lotus ponds, the multi-coloured flower beds, graceful willows and majestic pine trees and splendid palaces. Fluttering in the shimmering rays of the golden sun were busy fairies making every arrangement to ensure that the birthday party in the evening would go beautifully. Thousands of guests were invited to the paradise to share the joyous occasion with the goddess. The eight immortals were among the long list of guests.

The party went on very well indeed. There were laughter and joyous greetings throughout the evening. Fragrance and music filled the air. The shimmering moonbeams and the pleasant breeze added to the congenial atmosphere. At the end of the party the goddess sent her guests off personally with a gift each of a longevity peach.

The eight immortals enjoyed themselves thoroughly and many of them had taken quite a substantial amount of fine wine and good food. They were quite reluctant to return to the Isles of the Blessed. However, all great parties had to come to an end and so they left the western paradise.

On their way back the immortals had to cross the sea. Lu Dong Bin suggested that they each demonstrated their individual style and method of crossing the perilous water instead of crossing together in a boat. The others agreed as they were still flushed with the warmth of wine and in a playful mood.

Cao Guo Jiu used his castanets as a wooden boat. Zhong Li Quan floated on his magic fan. Lu Dong Bin put his sword horizontally on the water and stood firmly on it as it moved across the sea. Zhang Guo Lao took out a paper mule from his pocket, blew a breath of air on it and turned it into a mule that floated swiftly. He Xian Gu calmly put her lotus flower on the water and it grew large enough to carry her across the sea. Han Xiang Zi rode on his magic flute and hurried across the water. Li Tie Guai leaned on his crutch. Lan Cai He put his flower basket on the water. The basket sparkled in the water and caught the attention of the dragon king's mother who wanted to possess the beautiful flower basket. She caused the waves to rise in the most unusual way so that the basket dropped into the sea and Lan Cai He was imprisoned. The other immortals were furious. They descended immediately into the depths of the sea to the undersea kingdom to rescue their friend.

Upon their arrival the immortals found that the dragon king was holding a big feast at his glittering crystal-like palace to celebrate his mother's birthday. All the dragon king's ministers and subjects were taking their turns to present their gifts and well wishes. One of the outstanding gifts was a magic mirror. It was this mirror that reflected the image of Lan Cai He's glittering basket and tempted the dragon king's mother to capture it, as she was told that if she ate the flowers all her wrinkles would disappear.

As the Immortals approached the crystal-like palace they were stopped by a host of sea creatures wearing uniforms with the word 'guard' embroidered on them.

'Hi! Stop there. Who are you? You cannot stay here, you have to leave immediately,' the guards said.

'Set free our brother, Lan Cai He, and return his basket immediately,' the immortals demanded.

At that juncture, the water in the sea whirled and rippled as sea creatures attacked the immortals from all directions. The immortals found that the turbulent waters were like a swarm of hurricane cones hurling themselves with fury at them.

Meanwhile, in the palace, the dragon king's mother was most delighted as she held the glittering basket of flowers in her hands. She picked up one of the flowers and swallowed it. Immediately her wrinkles disappeared and the skin of her face was as smooth as that of a newborn baby. Everyone around her was joyous to witness the miracle.

By this time the immortals had already overcome the guards and were preparing to charge the palace. When the dragon king heard that the immortals were about to enter the palace he put on his armoured suit, mounted his dragon and came out of the palace with his soldiers to capture the intruders.

As soon as the dragon king caught sight of the immortals he blew a breath towards them. His breath turned into a cloud of black mist blurring their vision and choking their breath. Fortunately, Li Tie Guai managed to capture the threatening cloud with his magic gourd. The dragon king threw his magic sword towards his opponents but Lu Dong Bin was fast in defence, thrusting his glittering sword upwards to engage the King's powerful sword. More sea creatures charged forward to attack the immortals and Cao Guo Jiu threw his castanets at them killing a few of the attackers. Zhong Li Quan then waved his magic fan from side to side and the rest of the attacking sea creatures disappeared without a trace. Another host of sea monsters charged forward. But Zhang Guo Lao created strange rhythms with his wooden drum and the monsters reeled in pain. The dragon king was getting quite impatient with his unwelcome guests and he breathed a trail of fire towards them. But He Xian Gu threw a lotus flower towards him and his fiery breath turned to ashes which dissolved in the ice-cold water of the deep sea.

As the immortals were fighting for their lives the dragon king's son appeared in full armour. He shouted insults at the immortals and threw a spear at Han Xiang Zi who warded it off with his flute. As soon as Han Xiang Zi started to blow his magic flute the sea was turned into a turbulent whirl of water. All the sea creatures including the dragon prince were dazed and fell one by one in a faint. The entire palace was in darkness and everything was in confusion.

After a while the water grew calm again. But, to the dragon king's dismay and sorrow, he found his son dead and his army reduced to half. He left his palace in a rage and went straight to the heavens to complain against the immortals. Upon hearing the sad tale from the dragon king the Jade Emperor sent his representative, the goddess of the western paradise, to investigate the case. Thus, the goddess summoned the immortals and the dragon king for a thorough explanation. After she had heard both sides of the story she demanded a truce as both parties had erred. Lan Cai He was released and the eight immortals returned to their Isles of the Blessed in the Eastern Sea.

The Ten Suns

Whenever I lie down on the sun-kissed grass and think of the earth's firmness, the air's purity, the seas' glory and the sun's brilliance my mind is filled with the fantasy of the story of the sun goddess's ten sons.

It was the reign of Yao during the twenty-fourth century B.C. The people were happy and contented because their emperor was wise and compassionate. Early in the morning the farmers ploughed the fields with the hope of good harvest, the hunters took their dogs to the forests with the expectation of bringing home their best catch and womenfolk carried pails of clothing to the riverside with a song on their lips. As these happy people carried out their routine jobs the sun slowly crept above the mountain peak, piercing the veil of clouds, bringing warmth and cheer to the hardworking people and filling their hearts with hopes and dreams.

Although the people felt and enjoyed the sun every day they knew little about the sun. They could not imagine that there were as many as ten suns. These suns were the children of the heavenly king and the sun goddess. They lived under a huge tree with golden leaves that twinkled in the gusty breeze that swept over the top of a celestial mountain. They took turns to appear on the sky, or else it would be so hot that everything on earth would burst into flames.

One day the youngest and the most mischievous of the suns came up with an idea. He suggested that he and his brothers visited the earth together. Although the eldest brother was not keen on the idea in case trouble might occur he eventually was persuaded to join his brothers and so the ten suns appeared together in the sky.

The ten suns that rose above the misty mountain created an arc of fire scorching the earth, setting every combustible material on fire, drying every well and stream, making every living thing wither and threatening every life. Soon the lakes dried up, the paddy was destroyed, the earth cracked and people began to die. Screams, cries of desperation and weak pleas for mercy were heard everywhere. The wise men were seen on their knees in prayer. The emperor too fervently prayed to the heavenly king for help.

The heavenly king heard the fervent prayers and knew that he had to punish his sons. So he summoned his best archer, Hou Yi, and ordered him to do something to rescue the people on earth. Hou Yi took his magic bow and quiver of arrows and went to the earth with his wife. He climbed up the highest hill and saw the suns in the sky. He entreated them to return to their home but they would not listen. Hou Yi had little choice but to shoot down the suns before the earth was completely destroyed. One by one he shot his magic arrows. One by one the suns fell into the ocean until finally only one sun was left in the sky.

The immense heat broke up, and in its place came the soothing breezes. The scorching fire subsided, and in its place came a shower of rain. Soon even the remaining sun went down the mountain. The evening stars began to glitter. The birds that survived returned to their nests. The lost sheep

With his magic bow, Hou Yi shoots down nine of the ten suns.

found their way home. On the sidewalks and the streets people embraced each other with tears of joy. The once stagnant earth came back to life.

Hou Yi and his wife returned to the palace of the heavenly king to find him in grief, mourning for the death of nine of his sons. In a fit of anger he banished Hou Yi and his wife from the heavenly paradise. Hou Yi's heart sank to the ground. He pleaded for mercy but the heavenly king turned away. So Hou Yi and his wife became mortals and took refuge on earth.

Although Hou Yi and his wife were treated with respect and kindness by the people on earth, the couple could not help but yearn for the paradise they used to know so well. There they used to sail on the sacred river along banks of incense-bearing trees. In the gardens of paradise there were smooth green lawns with multi-coloured blossoms of magic flowers that bloomed for thousands of years. There angels sang and danced joyfully. Everything was full of life and every one was young because there was no time, no aging and no illness.

'We are mortals now. We will age and die. What a horrible thought!' said Hou Yi's wife, Chang E.

'Don't worry I'll think of something,' said Hou Yi.

'I heard that there is a herb on Kun Lun Mountain that gives eternal life to people. Could you get it for us please?' pleaded Chang E.

So Hou Yi left his home on his white steed and went to Kun Lun Mountain to look for the herb of immortality, planted in a garden belonging to the goddess of the western paradise. The goddess took pity on him and gave him the herb.

Hou Yi was received with open arms by his wife on his return. But his fatigue overcame him and he fell asleep as soon as he lay down on his bed. Chang E, who was very excited, took the herb from under Hou Yi's pillow and had a good look at it. The herb smelt so fragrant that she could not resist the temptation of tasting the herb. As soon as she swallowed the herb she felt a sense of weightlessness and relief. She felt as if she had wings. Then she began to float, higher and higher into the sky.

Soon Chang E reached the moon. There was not a soul on the moon. Chang E realized then that she had been too hasty in swallowing the herb and she had no choice but live an eternal life of loneliness. To this day the Chinese still pray to the lonely lady in the moon during the mid-autumn harvest festival.

Lunar New Year

To Chinese the most important day of the year is the first day of the lunar year. Chinese all over the world celebrate the Lunar New Year for a duration of fifteen days. But preparations for the celebrations can take as long as a month as families spring clean their homes with bamboo leaves to sweep away bad luck, give the walls a fresh coat of paint, make new curtains and clothes and spend many long hours baking biscuits, sweets and cakes. New posters of the door gods and chun lian *(New Year greetings and poems) are pasted on doors and walls respectively.*

On the eve of the New Year all members of the family from near and far try to be home for a reunion dinner for which a great feast is prepared. Food and fruit of good symbolism are eaten so that throughout the year people will enjoy good luck, health and success. The young stay up late so that their parents will live a long life.

On the first day of the New Year the gods of heaven are welcomed to earth and the homes through prayers and offerings. Auspicious greetings are exchanged, red packets for the young and gifts of oranges for the elders are given. Throughout the fifteen days relatives and friends visit each other's homes. Dragon and lion dances and street operas are staged to usher in luck and wealth.

Why do the Chinese celebrate Xin Nien (New Year)? What is the meaning of Nien? The following is a story which relates the origin of the Lunar New Year.

Thousands of years ago there was a lovely and peaceful town in China where people worked very hard and yet had time to relax over tea and tell a few tall tales in the evening. During summer, young and old alike remained outdoors until the sun went down, enjoying the warmth of the sun, the sweet smell of grass and the fresh, invigorating air. The youth cavorted in the meadows while little children recited sweet nursery rhymes as they sat on the laps of their grandparents. During the bitter cold of winter, the people stayed indoors and warmed themselves at the hearth, drinking pots of hot tea or warm wine. Those who had to be out would stop at the inn for a few cups of wine to keep their body warm on the journey home. Some would linger to while away the idle winter days. It was towards the end of one such winter that something terrible happened to the town.

Most of the townsfolk were indoors. The biggest inn in town was full, with some men drinking wine, some having tea, everyone talking and laughing. Suddenly, they heard a loud roar. Before they realized they were in imminent danger, a monstrous looking beast leaped in and appeared before them. The poor innocent people did not even have a chance to take a proper look at the wild beast before they were killed and devoured. Everyone was eaten except a young boy who fainted and fell under a table after he had taken one good look at the monster.

By the time the boy came to, the beast had already disappeared, leaving a trail of blood. The entire town was alerted and those who lost their loved ones were in deep sorrow. Bitterness and anger filled the hearts of many. Search parties were organized but the monster was not in sight. The

The marauding monster, Nien.

entire town was quiet, in deep mourning for those who lost their lives. The streets were deserted in the evenings. Doors were locked. Even windows were closed. The winter was like an eternity.

However, spring came, bringing with it much life, and the meadows were green again. The swallows soared above the fields strewn with tiny flowers. More people were on the road as men began to prepare their fields for sowing. Slowly people forgot the unhappy past.

Then, once again, it was winter time. Some people still remembered what had happened during the previous winter. But there were others who had forgotten. The bitterly cold weather was difficult to endure without some good warm wine and hot food. The inns were full even in the evenings. Then, the monstrous beast struck again. It attacked the noisy laughing crowd at one of the inns. Again, there was only one survivor who saw the beast. He swore that it fitted the description of the killer monster which appeared in the previous winter.

'We must do something about this. We just can't let it keep coming back and killing us!' shouted the leader of the clansmen.

'We will fight this monster. We will not sleep until we have caught it!' echoed the men who gathered in the market square.

The entire town was on the ready. Every man and youth was out in the street holding whatever weapon he could find. There were hundreds of men in full alert. They waited and waited. They spent days and nights in the streets but the monster, which they called Nien, never appeared. The men were exhausted. They were at a loss what to do. So they visited the wise men and asked them for advice.

'Did you not notice that it appeared at the end of winter this as well as last year? Take a rest, young men. The monster will not come again until the end of next winter. Prepare yourselves and wait for it to turn up. Take it by surprise when it comes again,' advised the oldest of the wise men.

'What shall we do and how do we prepare ourselves?' asked the youngest man.

'You know the colour red repels evil. Booming sounds from the gongs shakes one's confidence. Red banners distract attention. Fire crackers frighten living things. Go, get yourselves prepared,' said the wise man.

Spring came followed by summer and autumn. Once again it was winter time. The townsfolk had waited anxiously for that particular winter. They did not even feel the cutting wind. They did not mind the dark grey sky. They had toiled hard in preparation for the appearance of the monster, Nien. There was only one thing on their minds now: to destroy the monster.

On the day of winter which the monster had appeared previously all the children and women stayed indoors while the men gathered in groups and guarded the town. Every minute was like a day. Every shadow was like an omen. Some men held swords. Some grasped sticks. Some had fire crackers and a torch in their hands. Some stood before huge drums with sticks in their hands. Some carried huge red banners while others held gongs.

Suddenly there was a flash of light followed by a loud roar. A huge monstrous looking beast with round fiery eyes and a large bloody mouth appeared from nowhere. Its paws were huge and strong, its back muscular and flanked by a pair of wings. It leaped at a group of men holding swords. Before it could wield its power over the men hundreds of gongs sounded, hundreds of swiftly waving red banners surrounded it, hundreds of crackers fired at it and hundreds of men rushed towards it forming a circle with their swords. The monster screamed in fright. It could not open its eyes because of the firing crackers and the waving red banners. Its huge paws reached for its ears as the drums and gongs sounded loudly. It leaped up and disappeared as suddenly as it appeared. The men were joyous and they raised their arms in triumph.

'The old Nien has gone. It won't dare to come back again. Let us celebrate. Let us rejoice for we shall have a new era!' shouted the chief of the clansmen.

The victory celebrations took many days as the people visited each other, exchanged gifts, staged dances and enjoyed sumptuous meals.

Na Zha

During the reign of the tyrannical and dissolute Shang emperor, Zhou Wang, a wonder child was born to a military officer stationed at Chentang, an important access town to the imperial city. Said to be created by a unicorn, this child, Na Zha, was later deified.

Li Zeng already had two grownup sons when his wife Yan Shi was with child again. His elder son, Jin Zha, and his second son, Mu Zha, assisted him in the training of the army. An upright man, Li Zeng was worried about the future of his country which was disintegrating under the rule of a tyrannical emperor more interested in the pursuit of pleasure than the affairs of the state. However, he was much comforted by his two sons who were growing up to be tall, strong, courageous and dependable.

The pregnancy had reached its full term, and yet Yan Shi was not in labour. The physician was called in and herbs were taken to induce labour, but to no avail. It was a full year before the labour pains came. It was a difficult birth – the midwife was with Yan Shi a whole day and night before it was born. It was a huge ball of flesh. The attending maids screamed at the sight

Na Zha, the wonder child of a military officer, is said to be created by a unicorn.

and caused Li Zeng to dash into the bed chamber. It had rolled onto the floor, a red ball of flashing light. Li Zeng immediately drew his sword and sliced the ball neatly in half, thinking it was a demon.

No sooner had he done so than out jumped a radiant little boy wearing a red vest, and a golden bangle in his right hand. He smiled brightly at the incredulous Li Zeng. A red mole, as bright as a ruby, sat between his brows. Li Zeng again raised his sword high to strike at this demon in disguise, or so he thought. But his wife shouted from the bed, 'No! This is our son! How can you kill our son!'

'How do you know this is our son and not a demon that has gone into you? We cannot let this...this creature live!' Li Zeng remonstrated. But he had brought the sword down to his side although it was still unsheathed.

'How can this sweet little thing be a demon? Of course it is our child. He must be a gift from the gods. Please let him go!' his wife begged. And Li Zeng relented. He decided to call the boy Na Zha.

A few days after Na Zha's birth, Li Zeng had a Daoist visitor of unusual characteristics. He had grey hair but his facial features were like those of a youth. He introduced himself as Tai Yi Zeng Ren from the Golden Light Cave and expressed his desire to take Na Zha as his disciple as soon as he was ready to learn *wushu*. Li Zeng agreed and the Daoist left, riding on a cloud.

When Na Zha was seven years old he was two metres tall and possessed unusually immense power. A mischievous child, he was always getting into scrapes because of his great curiosity and his love of fun. He also loved to swim in the river and sea. One hot summer day he left home without informing his parents and went to the bank of the Jiu Wan He, a river with crystal clear water which twisted and turned like a centipede. The scenery beyond the river was like a painting. Na Zha was delighted. He jumped into the clear, cool water to take a swim. He took off his magic vest and waved it in the water not knowing that it had such magical powers that it rocked the stability of the undersea kingdom of the dragon king.

The dragon king and his subjects were confused and shaken, so an investigator was sent to find out who was causing the tremors on the sea bed. The investigator discovered that the mischief maker was just a child so he challenged him to a fight. Na Zha had never before seen a sea creature as grotesque as the investigator so he teased him for a while before he killed him with his magic bangle.

Other sea creatures who saw how easily Na Zha ended the life of the investigator quickly swam back to report to the dragon king. The third son of the dragon king, after hearing that it was a mere child who killed the investigator, volunteered to deal with the trouble maker. He led a team of sea creatures to the river and found Na Zha playing with his vest in the water. He shouted at him and charged forward, followed by his soldiers. But none of them was a match for Na Zha. Before long the third son of the dragon king was overpowered by Na Zha. He turned into a black dragon and Na Zha killed him with his bare hands.

The dragon king was furious and bitterly sad over the loss of his son. He reported the matter to the Jade Emperor of Heaven and went to see Li Zeng himself, demanding that Na Zha paid for his wrongdoings with his life. Li Zeng pleaded for mercy but the dragon king could not be placated. To save his parents from blame and punishment from the Jade Emperor, Na Zha surrendered to the dragon king who punished him by having his flesh scraped from his bones. Na Zha's soul took shelter with his martial master, Tai Yi Zeng Ren, who recreated him from the stalks and leaves of the lotus plant. Na Zha was further armed with a spear and a pair of wheels which gave out fire and wind bringing him to any destination within minutes.

After his death, Na Zha appeared before his mother in a dream. In the dream he told his mother that he was a wandering soul with no home, and requested that a shrine be built for him so that he had a place to go home to. So his mother built a temple in his honour on the legendary Mount Kingfisher Screen.

The Huanghe Formation

Feng Shen Bang *is a classical novel written during the sixteenth century towards the end of the Ming dynasty by Zhong Shan Yi Shou and Xu Zhong Lin. Based on events that took place during the Shang period and the beginning of the Zhou dynasty, it told of the cruel and unpopular rule of Zhou Wang and related how the warlord Wen Wang overthrew the tyrannical emperor. Feng Shen Bang was divided into one hundred sections, each filled with exciting and action-packed events and episodes. The most exciting of all, the chapter on the setting up of the Huanghe formation, is retold here.*

In the quiet of the countryside by the beautiful Wei river, Jiang Zi Ya often sat and held his fishing rod in pensive mood. Villagers passing by always wondered why he never put any bait on the rod and why he held it just above the waters of the river.

'I am not trying to catch fish but am waiting the arrival of a great leader who I can help,' Jiang Zi Ya explained. Villagers found him friendly and kind. Although his hair and beard were silver and his age was almost eighty, Jiang Zi Ya's spirit and vitality was like that of a youth. Very few people knew he was

彩云仙子大战黄天化曹勇画

Cai Yun Xian Zi throws her magic pearl at Wang Tian Hua and blinds him.

51

a pugilist and a geomancer, one who could foretell the future and assess situations with reference to cosmic forces. No one knew he was a beloved disciple of Yuan Shi Tian Jun, a hermit of extraordinary *wushu* feats who lived on the mighty Kun Lun Shan.

The political climate of the time was oppressive. The ruler, Zhou Wang, was a tyrant and an unpopular emperor who spent pots of gold on women and wine and emptied the country's treasury on buildings and luxuries for his amusement. Feudal lords such as Wen Wang were disgusted with the tyrant.

After waiting patiently for eight years, Jiang Zi Ya finally met Wen Wang who appointed him his prime minister. Jiang Zi Ya planned and fought many battles for Wen Wang during one of which he killed Zhao Gong Ming, one of the ablest warriors of Zhou Wang. Zhao Gong Ming had three sisters, Yun Xiao, Bi Xiao and Qiong Xiao, together known to all as San Gu (Three Sisters). To avenge the death of their brothers, San Gu challenged Jiang Zi Ya to a battle to the death. San Gu were assisted by Cai Yun Xian Zi and Han Zhi Xian. On the side of Jiang Zi Ya were Yang Jian, Wang Tian Hua, Mu Zha and Jin Zha.

In the midst of battle, Cai Yun Xian Zhi threw a magic pearl at Wang Tian Hua. Taken by surprise, Wang Tian Hua fell from his *qilin* (horse-like animal) as he was hit and blinded. Seared with pain, Wang Tian Hua thought that he was about to perish. Fortunately Jin Zha saw him and rushed forward to rescue him in the nick of time.

Meanwhile, Jiang Zi Ya attacked Yun Xiao fiercely and, having the upper hand, charged towards her. But Bi Xiao was quick to respond and rescued Yun Xiao just in time. Yang Jian lost no time in throwing his magic dog at Bi Xiao who screamed in pain as the magic dog tore off the skin on her shoulder.

Han Zhi Xian, realizing the dangerous situation, opened

Jiang Zi Ya attacks Yun Xiao fiercely.

her magic wind bag which let out a gust of black turbulent wind towards Jiang Zi Ya. At the same time Cai Yun Xian Zi let go her magic pearl which struck Jiang Zi Ya in the eye. Jiang Zi Ya fell from his bull-like horse in great pain. Yang Jian rushed forward and rescued Jiang Zi Ya before he could be further harmed.

Realizing that they should not stay any longer in the battle, Yang Jian and the other warriors took Jiang Zi Ya and Wang Tian Hua back to their camp. Fortunately, they had some excellent medicine for badly injured eyes. So Jiang Zi Ya and Wang Tian Hua were treated and had a speedy recovery.

Meanwhile, San Gu felt triumphant although they had minor injuries. They vowed never to rest until they had taken revenge on Jiang Zi Ya by taking his life. They recruited another six hundred soldiers and together with their assistants set up the Huanghe formation. Their plan was full of intrigues, booby traps and magical spells. The twists and turns were ninety-nine in number and thunder and lightning dispelled the desolate stillness of the formation sending intruders flying in the air like fallen leaves. Mortals could be turned to nothing and immortals cast into miserable beings. Indeed this magical formation of deadly spells was a formidable fort to Jiang Zi Ya and his warriors.

After training the soldiers and preparing them for the Huanghe formation, San Gu held an audience with Wen Tai Shi their strategist and superior. They also held a feast in celebration of their earlier victory over Jiang Zi Ya.

Wen Tai Shi was delighted with the Huanghe formation. He gave orders for another battle against Jiang Zi Ya. Riding on the back of a black *qilin* and flanked by his warriors, Wen Tai Shi and San Gu reached the approach to Jiang Zi Ya's camp and challenged him to another battle.

Jiang Zi Ya and Yang Jian responded by charging out of their camp towards the battleground within the Huanghe formation. As they entered the battleground they could see hundreds of soldiers waving flags and pounding drums amidst mysterious mists and fascinating lights. Cold howling winds cut the faces of Jiang Zi Ya and Yang Jian. Choking smoke blinded their eyes and blurred their vision. Hysterical screams and mysterious shadows distracted their attention. They were intrigued and confused. But Jiang Zi Ya and Yang Jian charged forward galloping at top speed along the tortuous paths.

The first duel inside the Huanghe formation was fought between Yang Jian and Qiong Xiao. Yang Jian tried to secure his position by raising his sword swiftly and with a swing thrust it at Qiong Xiao's neck. But the latter responded quickly warding off the sword with her magic box, which caused a shower of sparks. She then opened the magic box and a flash of lightning blinded Yang Jian momentarily. Before he could gallop off he was drawn into the magic box. Jin Zha saw the tragic incident and he tried to rescue Yang Jian by jumping on to the magic box and grasping on to its lid. Suddenly the lid opened emitting a blast of black poisonous cloud. Jin Zha was overcome by the thick suffocating cloud. Then he lost consciousness and was also trapped in the formidable magic box.

Jin Zha's brother, Mu Zha, was filled with apprehension when he saw with his own eyes how powerful the magic box was. But his courage was not diminished. He proceeded into the battle front to confront Qiong Xiao. He demanded that she released his brother and the others trapped inside the magic box. Qiong Xiao laughed at him and challenged him to a duel. Mu Zha wielded his magic sword and threw it at the magic box. A flash of lightning was followed by a thunderous blast. To Mu Zha's disappointment his sword broke into two and, before he could run away, he was drawn towards the magic box. He tried to resist but in vain and so he too was trapped inside the magic box.

At this juncture, Yun Xiao was full of confidence so she spread out her glittering magic wings and flew towards Jiang Zi Ya, swift as lightning. Just as she was about to attack Jiang Zi Ya, the latter ducked and galloped off at full speed. Qiong Xiao joined her sister in their attempt to capture Jiang Zi Ya. She put up her magic box and opened it wide. Jiang Zi Ya realized the danger so he spread out his magic yellow flag which emitted golden rays of energy to counter the evil spell of the magic box. Each of the rays transmitted powerful electrifying energy that sounded like crashes of a million pieces of metal and a million ringing bells. But the magic flag was no match to the evil power of the magic box and so Jiang Zi Ya was defeated. Fortunately, before he was harmed he escaped to his camp.

Back in the camp Jiang Zi Ya had a lengthy discussion with one of his advisors, Ran Deng, a knowledgeable Daoist. Ran Deng realized that the magic box was harmful to the captured warriors and could destroy them physically. He volunteered to make an attempt to rescue the warriors.

Early in the morning of the following day Ran Deng rode to the battle field of the Huanghe formation and challenged Yun Xiao to a duel. The crafty Yun Xiao led Ran Deng into one of the twisted paths of the Huanghe formation. There Ran Deng was suddenly attacked by a swarm of bees. For a moment he was dazed but, realizing that he was in a precarious position, galloped off as fast as he could. He was aware that by then a total of twelve of Jiang Zi Ya's warriors had been trapped either in the magic box or the booby traps of the Huanghe formation. He returned to Jiang Zi Ya's camp and suggested to him that they sought help from their master on Kun Lun Shan. Jiang Zi Ya agreed and Ran Deng left immediately.

On arrival at Kun Lun Shan, Ran Deng learnt that Yuan Shi Tian Jun, their master, had already left for Xiqi and would probably visit Jiang Zi Ya. So he immediately rushed back.

As Jiang Zi Ya and Ran Deng prepared to welcome their master they heard the wonderful sound of music in the air and then saw a chariot descending from the sky. The glittering chariot was borne by nine dragons preceded by white storks and followed by phoenixes of multi-coloured feathers. On the left and right of the chariot were young fairies playing flutes which filled the air with heavenly melody.

Yuan Shi Tian Jun descended from the chariot as Jiang Zi Ya and Ran Deng knelt to welcome him. The Daoist master and his disciples were brought into the main hall in the camp.

The following day Yuan Shi Tian Jun, accompanied by Jiang Zi Ya, went to the battleground of the Huanghe formation and declared war on San Gu. The three sisters appeared, looking triumphant. Yuan Shi Tian Jun wasted little time and, riding his flying chair, flew right into the dark interior of the Huanghe formation where he saw the twelve warriors lying on the ground in a trance-like state and near death. He knew he could not bring them back to consciousness so he decided to leave. At that moment Cai Yun Xian Zi hurled her magic pearl at him. But before the deadly pearl could reach the Daoist, it burst into powder and turned into dust. Cai Yun Xian Zi was shaken and she ran off as fast as she could.

Yuan Shi Tian Jun returned to Jiang Zi Ya's camp to find that his superior, Lao Zi, had arrived riding on a bull. On hearing what had happened, Lao Zi smiled and told Jiang Zi Ya to prepare for a duel with the three sisters.

The next day Lao Zi and his disciples rode to the battle front and asked San Gu to come forward. The three sisters dared not confront Lao Zi directly as they knew his might. Instead they hurled their magic flying scissors at Lao Zi hoping to behead him. Lao Zi was not at all excited. He waved his sleeve gently and the flying scissors disappeared into thin air. Shocked, the three sisters opened their powerful magic box, turning it towards Lao Zi who gently raised his right hand, causing the magic box to burst into flames and burn itself into ash. The three sisters screamed in utter frustration. Yuan Shi Tian Jun clapped his hands in joy. This maddened the three sisters so they charged at him in full speed. But he was well prepared. He took out a magic cup from his sleeve and threw it at the three sisters. It transformed itself into a huge cup emitting fire and electrical sparks. The three sisters were sucked into it. Screams of horror and agony filled the air as the sisters were churned into bits of flesh and pools of blood. As soon as they had disintegrated into nothingness, the Huanghe formation rocked like a volcanic mount and erupted amidst thunderous screams of terror. At last the Huanghe formation was destroyed.

Sworn Brothers
in the Peach Garden

It was the era of the Eastern Han (A.D. 25–220), the imminent end of a great dynasty, when corruption and decadence pervaded the empire. Taxes were increased to support the wanton extravagance of the imperial court. The rich exploited the poor and the poor suffered in silence. The empire was beginning to crumble in the face of misrule and the unrest and strife that resulted. Feudalism set in as warlords took advantage of the weak central government to carve little dominions of their own. It was during this time that there emerged three heroes who would be immortalized in legend and revered by the Chinese because of their great courage and their loyalty to the people. They were Liu Bei, Zhang Fei and Guan Yu.

During the period of the corrupt Eastern Han, in Hebei, at the village of Ju Lu, there lived three brothers. The eldest, Zhang Jiao, was a scholar and a thinker who, disgusted with the corruption and enraged by the exploitation of the common people, was determined to overthrow the government of the day. In this he was supported by his brothers, Zhang Bao and Zhang Liang who were equally outraged.

The three fearless brothers plotted and planned. Using

their wealth, they bought manpower and arms. In their hideout outside their village, they trained their men. Unfortunately, among their men, there was a traitor and an informer. For a small reward he revealed the three brothers' intentions and plans. Retribution was swift – an army was sent to eliminate the would-be rebels. Of the three brothers, only Zhang Jiao managed to escape, with a small band of followers. They took refuge in a mountain fortress not far from Ju Lu. The bravery of the Zhang brothers captured the imagination of the people and many young men travelled long distances to join Zhang Jiao and his fellow rebels.

In the meanwhile, the local magistrates in the county of Hebei posted proclamations on city walls and gateways for the arrest of Zhang and his men. In Zhuoxian, a small town in Hebei, the proclamations were posted everywhere. One day a distinguished-looking man with vivid eyes, a straight nose, and a square jaw was passing by the town gate when he saw such a proclamation on the wall:

> By order of the military commander and the Government, this county hereby make known that Zhang Jiao and his men are wanted. Any man who conceals him or his men or gives him help shall be deemed equally guilty. Whoever arrests and brings him forward, or offers information leading to his arrest, shall receive a reward of a hundred pieces of gold.

The distinguished-looking man was Liu Bei. Although he was of royal blood he was only a poor shoe vendor. He believed in doing an honest day's work for a hearty meal. And he was certainly not blind to the dishonesty and corruption of the ruling class. Pained by what he saw and by the sufferings of the ordinary folk, he yearned to take action. But he did not know how as he had no money nor an army.

Liu Bei read the proclamation carefully, touched by the heroic intentions of the rebels. He knew that they had made great sacrifices and were risking their lives for their countrymen. He sighed with regret and shook his head. Standing near by was another man with unusual facial features: large eyes, bushy eyebrows, a big fleshy nose, broad fleshy lips, and a bushy beard on his chin. This man stood tall and straight and he said with slight sarcasm, 'There is no cause for regret if you are not brave enough to serve the nation!' Liu Bei heard him and turned towards him in order to take a good look at him. He noted that he looked fierce but sincere so he introduced himself.

The tall man replied a little sheepishly not having expected Liu Bei to speak to him, 'I am a wine and pork vendor and my name is Zhang Fei.'

'Although I have little to offer, I would like to join these rebels and contribute in any way I can,' said Liu Bei.

'At this moment I, too, am quite prepared to offer all I have to help overthrow this decadent government. I have means and I am willing to spend my entire fortune to build up an army. Could we work together? Come, let's talk about it over a drink,' Zhang Fei invited, more excited by the minute.

At the tavern Liu Bei and Zhang Fei saw a strong and fine looking man pushing a cart before him. When he reached the tavern, the man stopped, and addressed them,

'Please may I have a bottle of wine? I am thirsty and I am in a great hurry. I am going to join the heroes of Zhang Jiao!' he added proudly.

Liu Bei took a good look at him and noticed that he had spirited eyes, a straight nose, firm lips and very large ears. He could not help but walk up to him and introduce himself. He then invited the man to drink with them.

'I am Guan Yu from Hedong. I detest these oppressive landowners. I am on the run for killing one bully five years ago.

Vowing to keep faith with each other – Liu Bei, Guan Yu and Zhang Fei.

I am trying to join Zhang Jiao and his men to bring back some decency to the country,' Guan Yu explained in between gulps of wine.

Thus the three men introduced themselves. However, they realized that the tavern was hardly the place to plan a rebellion and Zhang Fei invited the other two to his peach garden where they could discuss further.

Early the following day Zhang Fei tidied his peach garden and set up an altar with sacrificial food and drink. When Liu Bei and Guan Yu arrived Zhang Fei was delighted, for he was not sure if they would come. He suggested that they become sworn brothers and be united in achieving their goals of reforming and improving the nation's political situation. Liu Bei and Guan Yu agreed and the trio knelt and prayed. They swore to be blood brothers and prayed that they would die on the same day although they were not born at the same time. Liu Bei being the oldest was the big brother. Guan Yu was second while Zhang Fei was the third.

Hong Fu Nu and Li Jing

Hong Fu Ji *is a novel written during the Ming period by Zhang Feng Yi about three outstanding characters Li Jing, Hong Fu Nu and Qiu Ran Ke. The following extract relates how the three met.*

It was a chilly winter night. The icy-cold wind was howling like a wolf. The deserted streets were dark and full of shadows. Occasionally a lone drunken figure staggered down the shadowed lane and passed by Li Jing's humble house, the only one which was lit at this time of the night. Li Jing, a military strategist from a well known family, usually worked late into night.

Just as Li Jing was about to retire after a typically busy day he heard a soft knock on his door. He wondered who the caller could be at this late hour. The knock on the door sounded more urgent. Li Jing's legs took him automatically to the door and his right hand reached for the door latch, lifted it, and pulled the door open. He was dumbfounded by what he saw. Before him stood the most lovely young maiden he had ever seen, with spirited eyes and fine facial features.

With an air of ease and grace the young beauty spoke softly,

紅拂女送寒衣

夢霞寫

Hong Fu Nu presents Li Jing with a winter coat.

'Sir, my name is Hong Fu Nu. I have brought you a winter coat. Please may I come in?'

Li Jing, as if hypnotized, nodded his head again and again. Hong Fu Nu stepped into the house. Gazing into Li Jing's eyes she said, 'My mind is made up. I wish to serve you and always be at your side. Please do not send me away.'

He did not know how long they stood like that at the door, gazing into each other's eyes, but when Li Jing had gathered his wits, he found himself perspiring despite the cold draft blowing through the open door and realized that he was saying repeatedly that Hong Fu Nu was most welcome to stay with him. With a start, he moved aside for her to pass and then quickly closed the door to shut out the cold.

So it was that Hong Fu Nu came to live with Li Jing and took charge of the household chores in his home. A few days passed without anything unusual happening, except that Li Jing's life was much enriched by the gracious company of the capable and beautiful young maiden. But soon news came to Li Jing's ears that the family with whom Hong Fu Nu had lived and worked as a handmaiden of the mistress was greatly displeased and were threatening to have her punished once she was found. Li Jing and Hong Fu Nu talked over the matter carefully and decided that they had little choice but to run away.

They packed some essential clothing in their cloth bag and left without even looking back at the familiar little house where they had spent many happy moments together. They were determined not to be overcome by fear or threat.

After walking for some hours which seemed an eternity they arrived at an inn where they decided to take a rest.

Inside the inn there were few guests but one of them looked rather unusual. He had bushy eyebrows and vivid eyes. However, Li Jing and Hong Fu Nu did not notice his fierce looks at all. For they were horrified and unnerved by what they saw on his table: a human head and a human heart in a bag which seemed too small for the items it held. Li Jing and Hong Fu Nu felt as if something was stuck in their throats when the strange man took a bite of the heart and said with a grin, 'Don't look at me like this. This heart used to belong to a man without a conscience.'

The stranger then invited Li Jing and Hong Fu Nu to drink with him. Apprehensively, they sat down. The man said, 'Let me tell you. I have found the man who will be the next new Emperor.' After a short while the man left in a hurry. Li Jing and Hong Fu Nu then continued on their journey to the town Tai Yuan Cheng. Unexpectedly they met the strange man once again.

'It's good to see you again. Remember me? My name is Qiu Ran Ke. I am glad to see you again. Come with me. I will bring you to see the man who I know will be the next Emperor."

After a short journey the trio arrived at a humble-looking house where Qiu Ran Ke requested to see the master of the house, saying that he had something important to tell him. On seeing the man Qiu Ran Ke said to him, 'You are going to be our next Emperor.'

Qiu Ran Ke then turned to Li Jing and challenged him to make Li Si Ming emperor, offering to give all his wealth to Li Jing for the campaign. And so Li Jing, Hong Fu Nu and Qiu Ran Ke began on their campaign to make Li Si Ming emperor of a new dynasty, the Tang Dynasty.

.

The Burning of the
Red Lotus Temple

The Burning of the Red Lotus Temple *is a lengthy novel about
the adventures of four young pugilists, Lu Xiao Qing, Liu Chi,
Gan Lian Zhu and Chen Ji Zhi.*

Lu Xiao Qing, a young pugilist dressed in the clothes of a
scholar, was walking through the woods. It was getting late
and he was not sure where he could get shelter for the night.
So he kept a keen eye on any structure, no matter how humble,
where he could stop for the night. But there was none so he
kept walking on.

Humidity hung heavily over the woods as the sky was
overcast with dark clouds. To his relief Lu Xiao Qing heard soft
voices and faint footsteps approaching. He hoped that he
could get some information from the approaching strangers.

'Sirs, would you tell me where I could find an inn for the
night?' Lu Xiao Qing asked the group of men.

'There is no inn or private residence near by. The best place
you can stay in is the Red Lotus temple,' the oldest man among
the strangers who appeared to be farmers answered, pointing
at a path.

'Thank you,' Lu Xiao Qing said as he put his hands together

to show his appreciation.

Lu Xiao Qing's legs seemed to have recovered from fatigue and moved much faster than before. After half an hour, he spotted the roof ridge of a temple above some thick foliage and rugged rocks. He could see sculptured porcelain dragons flanking a miniature pagoda at the centre of the heavy roof ridge, below which was a gabled, sweeping, curved roof of green glazed tiles. This must be the Red Lotus Temple, Lu Xiao Qing thought to himself.

As he approached the temple, the walls below the roof became more visible. There were three pairs of red doors on the central wall. The centre pair of doors was closed and above them was a huge signboard with the words 'Red Lotus Temple' engraved on it. In front of the temple were two huge flag poles and by the sides, strategically placed, was a pair of fierce-looking stone lions. Lu Xiao Qing was glad that one of the side doors was half open. He pushed it ajar and walked into the courtyard of the temple. There was no one around so he walked on from one courtyard to another.

He finally found the main prayer hall from which he could hear murmuring and chanting of prayers. He did not wish to disturb any monk so he walked on to what he thought was the guest wing. Just as he was about to enter one of the chambers he sensed someone behind him. He turned and found a mean-looking monk scrutinizing him from head to toe. He realized that he owed the monk an explanation and so he spoke frankly about his intention.

'You can stay. Let me show you your room. My name is Zhi Ke Zeng,' said the monk.

Zhi Ke Zeng took Lu Xiao Qing to his room and had some vegetarian food served before he left. After a meal and a short rest Lu Xiao Qing felt refreshed. He tried to sleep but the fragrance of flowers and the moonlight in the courtyard tempted him to take a walk outside. He strolled casually and moved from one courtyard to another. Before he realized it he was approaching the courtyard of the main prayer hall. To his amazement and shock he saw a group of indecorously dressed women dancing and laughing in the court. Just as he was trying to figure out what was happening the women disappeared as quickly as they appeared. He returned to his room deep in thought. On arrival he found Zhi Ke Zeng waiting for him.

'How dare you try to poke your nose into our affairs. There is no choice for you but to become one of us or you will die!' the monk threatened.

'No way! You have no right to threaten me,' said Lu Xiao Qing.

Uneasiness prevailed and no one moved. Suddenly the monk jumped at Lu Xiao Qing with a short knife which he whipped out of his sleeve. Lu Xiao Qing defended himself and Zhi Ke Zeng retreated quickly, locking the door behind him. Lu Xiao Qing knew that the monk would return with more men. He tried to escape through the window but to his disappointment all the openings were grilled with iron rods. Just as he was at his wits' end, he heard a sound and looked up. The window at the top of one wall was slid open and against the dark sky was a darker figure.

'I have come to help you,' said the dark figure on the roof urgently. 'Quick, jump up, before the monk comes back.'

Lu Xiao Qing jumped up and moved as fast as he could trying to keep pace with the dark figure. They jumped down the wall onto the lane outside the temple and ran quickly into the forest. When they knew that they were not followed, they slowed to a walk and started talking.

'My name is Liu Chi. I have come here to rescue a great man who is imprisoned by the evil monks. I am the disciple of Jin Lao Han,' said the man in black.

Lu Xiao Qing introduced himself and related what had taken place and what he had seen in the temple. He then learnt that Liu Chi was looking for an important military official, Bu Wen Zheng. As he and Liu spoke, a group of soldiers approached and challenged them. They started to fight but the soldiers were no match for them.

When they had subdued the soldiers, Liu Chi demanded to know where they came from and what they were doing in the forest. The leader of the group replied that they were looking for their commander, Bu Wen Zheng. Liu Chi revealed that their commander had been captured by the monks of the Red Lotus Temple and urged them to return to their base and garner a big rescue party.

When the soldiers had scuttled off, Liu Chi brought Lu Xiao Qing to meet his two comrades, Chen Ji Zhi, a young man like himself, and Gan Lian Zhu, daughter of his master. Lian Zhu confessed to Lu Xiao Qing that she first saw him in the Red Lotus temple when Zhi Ke Zeng was trying to hurt him. She revealed that when the monk tried to stab him with his sharp knife she threw her flying needle at the monk's arm. Lu Xiao Qing then realized why Zhi Ke Zeng had left in a hurry, and he thanked Lian Zhu for helping him.

Lian Zhu also related that she saw with her own eyes Bu Wen Zheng's capture by a monk and a nun from the Red Lotus temple. Following them to the temple, she saw Zhi Yuan, the abbot, sitting on a round stage raised from the ground, wearing a yellow robe. Surrounding him were young women, some attending to his needs, some dancing. As soon as Bu Wen Zheng was brought before him, he dispersed the women and ordered his attendants to serve the military commander with wine and food. Then he turned to Bu Wen Zheng and urged him to join the Red Lotus Temple sect, threatening him with death if he did not. The military commander refused flatly. Angered and disappointed, Zhi Yuan had Bu Wen Zheng imprisoned inside a huge bronze bell in the temple dungeons so that in time he would starve and suffocate to death.

After hearing what Lian Zhu had said Liu Chi and Lu Xiao Qing were determined to return to the Red Lotus temple to rescue the military commander. Lian Zhu and Chen Ji Zhi decided to go with them.

When the four arrived at the external walls of the temple they used their *wushu* skills to jump up and then down the high formidable wall into the interior courtyard of the main prayer hall. They were immediately surrounded by monks who were armed to the teeth, and engaged them in a furious skirmish in which the monks found that they were no match for Lu Xiao Qing and company.

While the young men were busy fighting the monks, Lian Zhu ran down to the dungeons, lifted the huge bronze bell and rescued Bu Wen Zheng.

Meanwhile, the monks, realizing that they were fighting a losing battle, tried to run away. Some, together with the abbot, managed to escape before Bu Wen Zheng's army arrived.

The commander thanked his rescuers and ordered his men to search the temple and capture the evil monks. When he realized that the abbot had escaped, he told his men to raze the temple to the ground so that Zhi Yuan could not return to continue his immoral and unsavoury practices.

火燒
紅蓮寺
夢霞

The Red Lotus Temple is razed to the ground to prevent the immoral monks from returning.

Outlaws of the Marsh

This is a lengthy Chinese classical novel written as early as the 14th century by Shi Nai An and Luo Guan Zhong. Today there are many versions of the novel and contents vary from twenty-six to one hundred and twenty-four chapters. Written to record the atrocities of a corrupt and decadent government towards the end of the Yuan dynasty, it contains the adventures of one hundred and eight heroes and heroines, rebel leaders fighting against the oppressive government. The rebels stationed themselves on Mount Liang in Shandong and championed the cause of the poor and downtrodden. The stories that follow are about two of the more outstanding heroes, Lu Da and Lin Chong, who were admired for their compassion and courage.

Major Lu pummels Zheng Guan Xi

Shi Jin was quite impressed by the hustle and bustle of city life when he arrived at Weizhou. As he was tired from his long journey from Huazhou, he decided to have a drink and some food at an inn. When the waiter came with his order, Shi Jin asked if he knew a man by the name of Wang Jin, a *wushu* instructor. As the waiter was replying that he did not know him, a tall man with unusual attire entered the inn. Shi Jin was told to approach the tall man because he was the 'major' and he knew most of the instructors in the region. So Shi Jin introduced himself to the tall man and learnt that he was major Lu Da. From Lu Da he learnt that Wang Jin was in the Yanan garrison. Politely, he invited Lu Da to partake of the food with him.

After Shi Jin and Lu Da had drunk and eaten their fill, they strolled down the main street, where they met Li Zhong, also a *wushu* instructor, who was trying to peddle medicine on the street. The trio went to a tavern to have some wine. As they were settling down to a good time, they heard someone weeping in an adjoining room. Swiftly, without a word, they moved out of their cubicle to the room next door, where they found an old man consoling a young maiden who was weeping uncontrollably.

Upon enquiry, they learnt that the weeping maiden, Jin Cui Lian, was from the east. She and her parents had come to Weizhou to visit relatives. Unfortunately her mother fell ill and her father ran short of money. A local wealthy man named Zheng took hold of the opportunity to make her father sign a contract, exchanging her as a concubine for three thousand strings of cash. After three months she was driven out by Zheng's wife and her father was forced to return the money which was never given to him in the first place. Thus, she had to sing daily for money which was given to Zheng to pacify him. She was crying because her earning for the day was not sufficient to pacify Zheng and she could foresee her father being abused by Zheng.

Lu Da on hearing the touching story gave the maiden and her father, Jin, some money and advised them to leave for home. When the innkeeper tried to stop them from leaving, Lu Da gave him a beating, and so father and daughter left Weizhou with their belongings.

Lu Da was furious that Zheng should bully the weak. He went to the butcher shop owned by Zheng who recognized him as the major. Lu ordered him to prepare ten catties of lean meat, ten catties of fat meat, and ten catties of gristle all finely chopped. After Zheng had done what he was told Lu Da took hold of the chopped meat and threw it in Zheng's face. In a rage, Zheng grabbed his chopper and attacked Lu Da. But he was no match for Lu Da who subsequently beat him up before he left the city.

Lu Da Creates an Uproar on Mount Wutai

Lu Da came to the busy county of Yanmen where he heard a proclamation for his arrest being made by a man. It was then that he found out that Zheng had died afte the beating. There, too, he met the old man, Jin, whom he had rescued from Zheng.

Jin related to Lu Da how he and his daughter had fared since they parted; his daughter had become a concubine of a wealthy man named Zhao. Jin then brought Lu Da back to Cui Lian's house for a drink. When Zhao returned he was introduced to Lu Da. Zhao treated him with much respect as he was the benefactor of his beloved concubine. Lu Da was entertained by Zhao in his manor for a few days but his host realized with fear that he might be discovered by the military men. So Zhao advised Lu Da to take refuge at the monastery on Mount Wutai, of which he was a patron. Lu Da agreed, and he set out for the monastery accompanied by Zhao.

Upon their arrival at the gate of the monastery the deacon and supervising monks received Zhao and Lu Da with warmth and brought them to see the abbot. Zhao introduced Lu Da to the abbot as his cousin and expressed that Lu Da had the desire to become a monk. The abbot agreed to ordain him in spite of the elder monks' protests.

A couple of days later at the chosen auspicious time, in front of six hundred monks, Lu Da had his hair shaved to become a monk. He was given the religious name of Sagacious and was introduced to all the monks.

On the following day Zhao left for home after he had counselled Lu Da to be patient with others. Little did he know that soon after his departure Lu Da would refuse to follow the routine prayer and meditation sessions of the monastery. His misbehavior was reported to the abbot, but he did not think it necessary to impose punishment on him.

A few months passed by in which Lu Da did not create any untoward incident that demanded much attention from the rest of the monks – until one day when he walked out of the monastery without permission. On his way down the mountain he took a short rest in a pavilion. As he sat there resting, he began to feel sorry for himself, as he had been deprived of meat and wine since he entered the monastery.

Just as he was yearning for a drink, a wine peddler carrying two buckets of wine approached the pavilion. Lu Da wanted to buy some wine from the peddler, but he was told that the abbot would not allow monks to drink wine. Lu Da was furious that the peddler refused to sell him wine. He kicked him and then drank a great deal of wine from the buckets. The wine peddler gathered the half empty buckets and ran off as fast as he possibly could.

Lu Da was quite drunk as he walked back to the monastery. When he reached the gate he was stopped by the gatekeepers because they realized that he was drunk. Lu Da was so infuriated by their action that he beat up one of gatekeepers. In the meanwhile, the other gatekeeper had run away to make a report to the chief monk, who gathered a group of men armed with weapons to try and subdue him. Lu Da gave a thunderous cry and charged into the monastery. A fight would have ensued, but the abbot came on the scene in time. The abbot ordered Lu to behave and bade him take a rest. Lu was taken back to his room and he fell asleep at once.

The following morning Lu Da was admonished by the abbot and was told to reform. Lu Da solemnly promised not to leave the monastery without permission or misbehave again. However, after four months, he got restless again and could not resist the temptation to get out of the monastery. He went into town, to an ironsmith to have an iron staff made. He then went from one inn to another trying to buy some wine. After he was turned down a few times he was eventually given a great deal of wine to drink by an innkeeper because he was intimidated by Lu Da's belligerence. Then Lu Da also demanded to be served dog's meat. He was quite drunk by the time he made his way back to the monastery.

When he arrived at the pavilion on the side of the mountain, he was so drunk that he accidentally demolished half the beautiful pavilion. When he reached the gate of the monastery, he found that the gatekeepers had closed it. Angered, he destroyed two icons nearby before he pushed open the gate and staggered back to the monk's quarters. There the monks were in meditation. They were shocked to find Lu Da eating a dog's thigh and offering it to them. The entire gathering of monks was agitated and fled amidst chaotic disarray. The uproar was followed by an attack on Lu Da by two hundred monks armed with clubs and staffs. The monks were, however, no match for Lu Da, who fought fiercely and forcefully. The abbot came just in time to stop the fight before someone was killed, although several were already hurt.

The following day the abbot told Lu Da that he had to be transferred to another monastery as he had committed many deeds of mischief and caused the anger of the other monks. Lu Da bowed to show his respect before he left the monastery on Mount Wutai, his belongings on his back.

Lin Chong Accidently Enters the
White Tiger Sanctum

After Lu Da had left Mount Wutai he went to Xiangguo monastery where he was received and taken to see the abbot. Because of his errant background, he was asked to take charge of the vegetable garden and lived with the elderly monks.

Near the vegetable garden there was a gang of thieves who lived on money they obtained through stealing and selling vegetables from the garden. When Lu Da took on the task of garden keeper, the thieves thought that as he was new to the job they could bully him. But to their surprise Lu Da outwitted them and revealed his *wushu* skills. The thieves were completely convinced that Lu Da was their superior and they hero worshipped him. Everyday they brought him wine and meat and they ate together.

One day while Lu was demonstrating some *wushu* moves with his long-handled half-moon spear before the thieves and vagabonds, a *wushu* instructor named Lin Chong, who had silently appeared and observed his mastery, applauded him. Lu Da introduced himself to Lin Chong and learnt that the latter had come with his wife and maid to the temple of the monastery to offer joss and prayer. Though they had just met, Lu Da and Lin Chong felt like old friends and agreed to be sworn brothers. Just as they were conversing animatedly, Lin Chong's maid came running and reported excitedly that a young man was harassing her mistress. Lin Chong rushed off to rescue his wife. In anguish, he learnt that the bully was the adopted son of Marshal Gao Tai Wei and that he had to be patient in dealing with such an influential person. By then Lin Chong was quite beside himself with anger and wanted to take Gao to task, but he was restrained by his friends. So the incident appeared to be settled amicably.

However, Gao Ya Nei could not forget Lin Chong's wife,

Lin Liang Zi. A few days after the temple row, Gao Ya Nei was having wine with his friends and talking about Lin Liang Zi. His friends who saw an opportunity to win further favours from Gao Ya Nei devised a plan to help him get close to Lin Liang Zi.

On the chosen day one of the conspirators befriended Lin Chong and invited him to a drink. After a time, someone was sent to the inn that Lin Chong was lodging to tell Lin Liang Zi that her husband was drunk and needed her attention. She was then lured to a place where Gao Ya Nei was eagerly waiting for her. Fortunately Lin Chong was informed on time by one of Lu Da's vagabond friends, and he managed to rescue his wife from Gao Ya Nei who fled at his sight.

A pretty woman had twice escaped his clutches, where no other woman had ever done before. Gao Ya Nei was furious, seething with humiliation. He ranted and raved while his sycophants cowered in fear. Then one of them stepped forward bravely and, with as calm a voice as he could muster, said, 'The only way is to make Lin Liang Zi helpless by killing Lin Chong, and I know how we can do it.' And so a vicious plot was hatched, in which Gao Ya Nei's father, Marshal Gao Tai Wei, was drawn.

In order to obtain the cooperation of Marshal Gao, his son pretended to be very ill. As he was the only son and bearer of the Gao family name, Marshal Gao would do anything to make his son well again.

With that last piece of the plot in place, the trap was complete.

A man interested Lin Chong into buying a rare but excellently made sword from him. To help Lin Chong verify the quality of the sword, one of Marshal Gao's lieutenants invited him to the marshal's house so that they could compare this sword with his.

Lin Chong was led to Marshal Gao's house. They passed

through a series of courtyards before coming to a garden pavilion. Then the lieutenant left him to fetch his sword. Lin Chong waited, patiently at first, for the lieutenant. However, the man was taking a long time, and, running out of patience, Lin Chong decided to go in search of him. He went in the direction that the lieutenant had gone. After a time, he found that he had wandered into the White Tiger Sanctum where the most confidential of military matters were discussed. He sensed that something was wrong but before he could leave Marshal Gao was standing before him and roaring,

'How dare you enter this place without my permission. Look, you are carrying a sword. You have the intention to harm me.'

Before Lin Chong could explain Marshal Gao had given the order to arrest him. A big group of men swarmed into the room and surrounded Lin Chong. He was overpowered and by order of the Marshal was banished to Kaifeng to be tried and executed.

At Kaifeng Lin Chong pleaded not guilty. The prefect in charge of the case realized Lin Chong's innocence. However, fearful of Marshal Gao's power and influence, he had Lin Chong caned and exiled to Cangzhou.

Lu Da Makes Havoc in the Wild Boar Forest

Lin Chong was escorted by two soldiers to Cangzhou. Now, these two men were bribed by Marshal Gao to kill Lin Chong in the White Boar Forest. On the way, they ill-treated Lin Chong so that he became quite weak.

In time, Lin Chong and his escorts arrived at the White Boar Forest. As they entered the forest, veils of mysterious mist enveloped them. Old, gnarled trees with twisted branches stood like frozen witches haunting the entire area. Huge birds with strange cries circled in the sky as if waiting for new prey.

After walking a short distance, to Lin Chong's surprise, the escorts tied him to a tree. The men then showed their evil intention when they revealed that Marshal Gao wanted them to kill him. Just as they dealt the first blow on Lin Chong's head Lu Da appeared from behind a tree and stopped the escorts from their shameless deed. Lu Da was furious and wanted to strike the escorts with his spear. But Lin Chong stopped him from harming the escorts explaining that it was Marshal Gao who ordered them to kill him. Lu Da agreed to spare the escorts provided they carried Lin Chong, who was badly hurt.

Lu Da and Lin Chong, who was assisted by the escorts, walked for some distance before they arrived at a tavern where they took a rest and had some food. After dinner they continued on their journey to Cangzhou. After twenty days, the little party reached a village nearby Cangzhou. There, Lu Da took Lin Chong to a pine grove to take a short rest.

'My sworn brother, from here to Cangzhou the roads are quite busy and open. I don't think the wicked escorts could do much harm to you. So I'll say goodbye now and we will meet some time in the future,' said Lu as he handed some silver pieces to Lin Chong. He also gave some money to the escorts, warning them not to harm Lin Chong. The escorts assured him that they would not do anything foolish. Lu Da bade them goodbye and left.

Lin Chong Takes Shelter in the Mountain Spirit Temple

Lin Chong finally reached Cangzhou where he was handed to the prefect. Fortunately the prefect was kind to him – instead of sending him to the dungeons he sent him to the garrison prison temple to be a temple keeper. Lin Chong gave the prefect some money as a gesture of his gratitude.

Lin Chong was quite comfortable working at the temple.

He was allowed to come and go quite freely. One fine morning he took a walk and unexpectedly met a man whom he once helped from being punished for allegedly stealing money from his employer. Xiao Er was overjoyed to see Lin Chong and invited him home for a meal. From then on, Lin Chong frequently ate at Xiao Er's home at the latter's invitation. Xiao Er and his wife had saved up enough money to open a tavern where he sold his customers food and wine.

One day some men came to Xiao Er's tavern to drink and dine. They spoke in whispers and mentioned Marshal Gao in their conversation. Xiao Er overheard part of it and suspected that they had the intention of harming Lin Chong. When Lin Chong came to pay Xiao Er a visit that same day, Xiao Er warned him about what the men had said and would possibly do. From Xiao Er's description Lin Chong knew that the men were sent by Marshal Gao. As a precaution he bought a sharp dagger and kept it in his boot.

A few days passed by without any unpleasant incident. Instead, Lin Chong was told that he was to be given a better job at the army depot. The day he had to report to the new place of work was a very cold winter day. The wind howled, and swirled the snow into treacherous drifts. The sky was black with threatening clouds. Lightning ripped the sky and the thunder sounded like the sky crashing on to the earth. Lin gritted his teeth and held his fists tightly as he struggled to the depot. He went through the depot gate to the caretaker's hut where he found the old soldier who was to exchange duty with him.

The old soldier gave him some personal advice including where he could buy wine and food. Lin Chong thanked him and the old soldier departed. Lin Chong tried to settle down, but the hut was far from comfortable and was not insulated from the bitter cold outside. Shivering, Lin Chong braved his way to the market place to buy some wine. He was much relieved when he reached a tavern where he ordered some food and wine.

As he hurried back to the depot he found that the weather was even more severe than before. The snow-covered roads shimmered in the murderous darkness of the night. The howling wind felt like sharp knives slashing his numbed face. He walked as fast as he could, impatient to be home. However, to his dismay, when he arrived at the gate of the depot, he saw that the humble hut, his home, had collapsed. Nothing was visible except a heap of timber and a part of his quilt. Gazing at the sky and feeling a little lost he tried to figure out what to do next. He then remembered that there was a temple nearby. So he gathered whatever he had and walked to the temple hoping to spend the cold night there.

Lin Chong found that the temple, dedicated to the Mountain Spirit, was deserted. When he entered the temple hall he put down his belongings and shook the snow off his worn-out coat. Then, drawing his quilt around him, he tried to sleep. As he was beginning to doze off, he heard a loud cracking sound. Startled, he got up and looked out towards the direction of the sound. The depot was on fire! His first instinct was to rush out to the burning depot to put the fire out. However, he was stopped by voices of men outside the temple. Sensing danger, he hid behind the temple door and strained to hear what the men were saying. From their conversation, Lin realized that they were sent to burn down the depot and to kill him. If he should escape, he would be framed for the crime of burning down the depot. Lin Chong was overcome with anger and disgust. He charged at the men and, one by one, he killed them. He swallowed all the wine he had bought and left the temple.

Knowing that Gao Tai Wei would continue to hunt him down, Lin Chong decided to join the rebels on Mount Liang.

Wu Song Kills His Sister-in-law

One of the most popular characters in the Outlaws of the Marsh was Wu Song. Young, courageous, strong and just, his personality and his adventures were an inspiration to would-be heroes. One story told of how he overcame a man-eating tiger single-handedly and saved a whole town from death and fear, and then refused the rewards that the townfolk tried to shower on him. Another story of how he killed his ruthless sister-in-law has been dramatized and is a popular opera among the Chinese.

Wu Da Lang, a hawker selling buns in Guang Peng Prefecture in Qing He Xian, was the envy of most men in town because his wife, Pan Jin Lian, was the most beautiful woman for miles around.

Pan Jin Lian was a former maid of Pan Yuan Wai. She had offended her old master by refusing to be his concubine. So he married her to Wu Da Lang, the shortest and ugliest man in town.

A weak and undisciplined woman, Jin Lian yearned for the good things in life which her husband could never afford to provide. As it was, Wu Da Lang had to work very hard from morning until evening to sell enough buns to provide for her daily needs. Thus, he had very little time to keep her company. But this suited her fine because she dreaded the company of her ugly and silly husband.

The most idle and wealthiest young man in town was Xi Men Qing. He was good looking and was fond of beautiful women. He was attracted by Jin Lian's fine features and gentle manner. Even though she was a married woman, Xi Men Qing longed to possess her. So he gained the cooperation of the greedy matchmaker, Wang Po. As part of the scheme, Wang Po presented expensive gifts to Jin Lian, from Xi Men Qing, and conveyed to the vain young woman his praises of her beauty. Unable to resist the flattery or the expensive gifts, Jin Lian succumbed to the overtures of Xi Men Qing. She betrayed her husband.

A secret cannot remain a secret forever. One fateful day, Xi Men Qing was trying to slip into the home of Wu Da Lang when Yun Ge, a fruit seller, tried to sell him some fruit and earn a few coins. Yun Ge was roundly scolded by Wang Po while Xi Men Qing quickly entered the house. After Wang Po too had entered the house, the fruit seller, suspicious that such a rich man should visit a poor man's home and furtively too, moved silently to a window and looked in. To his dismay he saw Xi Men Qing eating and drinking with his friend Da Lang's wife. Angry for his betrayed friend, the fruit seller immediately reported the incident to Da Lang. Shocked and saddened, Da Lang was at wit's end over what to do. Then he decided: first, he would verify the truth of the story.

The next day, Da Lang returned home earlier than usual. And there they were, Xi Men Qing and his wife Jin Lian, in bed together. Enraged, he leapt towards Xi Men Qing, his fists high, ready to strike. But he was no match for Xi Men Qing who was trained in *wushu*. Da Lang was badly injured by his wife's lover.

The lovers, in their moment of panic, decided to kill Da

Lang. With the help of Wang Po the matchmaker, they poisoned the hapless bun seller, and buried him hurriedly.

By this time Wu Song, who was made constable after his heroic killing of the man-eating tiger, had completed his assignment in another prefecture and had just returned to Guang Peng. The first thing he did when he returned was to pay a visit to his brother, Da Lang. When he arrived at his brother's house he was overcome by shock and grief to find that his brother had passed away and was already buried. He was told by his sister-in-law that his brother suffered a strange but fatal illness that took his life. Hurling herself at Wu Song, the immoral widow pretended to be overcome by grief and distress.

To ease the pain in his heart Wu Song took a long walk alone. As he emerged from the forest onto the road leading back to the town, he met the fruit seller who, fearfully lest he was overheard, told Wu Song what he knew, and his suspicion that Da Lang was murdered. Mad with fury, Wu Song nonetheless knew that he had to be fair and decided to gather evidence before he brought the murderers to court. Exhuming his brother's body, he found that his brother was indeed poisoned: the bones had turned black as charcoal.

He immediately went to the magistrate. However, Xi Men Qing had seen the magistrate just before him, with a thousand pieces of gold. The magistrate refused to try the case, giving the excuse that there was no proof that the accused were at the scene of the crime. Also, there was no murder weapon, and the blackness of the bones was inconclusive evidence for murder.

Wu Song decided to take matters into his own hands. The following day Wu Song went to see Jin Lian and requested her to invite all her friends and relatives home to commemorate his brother's death. He personally invited Wang Po and a few neighbours. After the guests had been served food and drink, he made Jin Lian kneel before his brother's altar. Then, placing

87

the blade of his sword at her throat, he demanded that she made a full confession of what she had done. Full of shame and regret, Jin Lian related how she and Xi Men Qing became lovers and how they killed her husband when he found out about their affair.

Wang Po, more fearful by the minute as Jin Lian tearfully told her story, made to escape quietly. But Wu Song noticed her sidling towards the door and stopped her before she could get away. He tied Wang Po up, then, swiftly, he plunged his sword into Jin Lian's heart, thus avenging his brother's death. Cutting off her head, he left in search of Xi Men Qing.

At the Lion Bridge tavern, Wu Song found the man drinking and merry making with two songstresses. Xi Men Qing looked at Wu Song, fear in his heart. Wu Song charged at him and a fierce fight took place. After a long duel Xi Men Qing was defeated and was killed by Wu Song who cut off his head and placed it before his brother's altar.

Wang Po was dragged to the magistrate's court to face justice. Wu Song then gave himself up to be banished to the Dong Ping Prefecture to face judgement.

武松大戰西門慶攀霞咋

Wu Song duels with Xi Men Qing, his brother's murderer.

A Wild Cat for a Prince

*During the reign of the Song emperor Zhen Zhong (A.D. 998–1022)
when corruption was the order of the day and the wronged who
had no power or money had little or no recourse to justice, there
was a magistrate who courageously remained true to the principles
of fairness and justice at the peril of his own life. No wrongdoer,
not even an empress or princess's consort, could escape the jaws of
his tiger guillotine. It is no wonder that Justice Bao Qing Tian,
or Bao Gong, is today revered as a deity.*

Zeng Zhong the Song emperor had two lovely concubines Li
Chen Fei and Liu Fei who became pregnant at about the same
time. One mid-autumn evening Zeng Zhong was taking a
stroll in the imperial garden accompanied by his two expectant
concubines. The air was filled with the fragrance of autumn
flowers, the soft breeze refreshing, particularly after too much
wine.

The emperor's somnolent mind drifted from one pleasant
thought to another, and then dwelt on the imminent double
happiness of being a father twice over. He frowned suddenly
as he remembered what his astrologer had told him. He could
not quite understand what the astrologer had said, but knew

vaguely that the stars were not favourable to the impending births. So thinking, he called his two concubines to his side and, as they ambled over, took a silk pouch embroidered with dragons from his sleeve. Carefully, he took out two jade seals and gave one each to the imperial wives, for jade had the power to repel evil and protect the owner. From the bag, he also took out two golden balls inlaid with pearls and gave them to the delighted concubines.

'Keep these with you always,' enjoined the emperor. 'They will protect you.'

'Thank you, Your Majesty,' the beautiful women chorused. They then looked carefully at the exquisite jewels and found that on each of the golden ball was engraved most skilfully a name. One was Li and the other Liu. With a tone of authority the emperor announced, 'Whoever produces me a son first will be crowned empress.'

The following day the ambitious concubine Liu Fei summoned her uncle, a court official, the cunning and vicious Guo Huai.

'If Li Chen Fei should give birth first I'll never be empress. What should we do?' asked an agitated Liu Fei.

'Your gracious highness, my beloved niece, we must pull up the roots if we don't wish to see the plant grow and grow again. Kill her and her baby, then we'll have no more worries,' uttered the evil-hearted Guo Huai.

At that moment one of Liu Fei's court attendants, Kou Chu, passing by the inner chamber, overheard the conversation between uncle and niece.

'Oh dear, how on earth can they think of such an evil deed. I must try to help Her Highness Li Chen Fei,' Kou Chu thought to herself.

It was a fine day, and eunuchs of the imperial palace were busy running around preparing baskets of presents and food because it was the birthday of the emperor's eighth brother.

Zeng Zhong's trusted eunuch, Chen Lin, was sent out of the palace to present the gifts to the prince.

Li Chen Fei started to have contractions and went into labour. The emperor was joyous. The intensity of his happiness and excitement made Liu Fei more jealous than ever. Guo Huai whispered to her to do something about the situation before it was too late.

'Your Majesty, since Chen Lin is not around, should I help sister Li Chen Fei?' said Liu Fei trying her best to hide her true feelings.

'How generous you are. Indeed you should stay by her side in case she has problems,' answered the excited emperor.

Guo Huai went with his niece into Li Chen Fei's chamber together with the midwife who had been bribed. Chun Er, Li Chen Fei's personal maid, was sent away to help with the hot water and towels.

After hours of agonizing labour Li Chen Fei gave birth to a lovely baby boy. Perspiring with the exertion she had a brief glance of her son before she sank into a deep slumber. Liu Fei and Guo Huai quickly sprang into action: they wrapped the baby in a length of cloth, put him into a basket and smuggled him out of Li Chen Fei's chamber. Then they placed a dead wild cat beside Li Chen Fei. Kou Chu was summoned to take the newly-born prince out of the palace.

'Take this baby and throw him into the deep water below the Gold Water Bridge. Make sure no one sees you. Now swear you will never tell anyone what happens tonight or else...' Liu Fei hissed threateningly.

Kou Chu nodded her head nervously and then walked into the darkness feeling wretched. How could she kill this child, the future emperor? Tears streaming down her cheeks because she was afraid and did not know what to do to save the child, she walked towards the bridge. When she came to the bridge she gave a cry of despair for she could not bring herself to throw the baby into the fast flowing, icy cold stream, yet was terrified of the consequences of not obeying her mistress's command.

A shadowy figure emerged from the darkness towards her, attracted by her cry. It was Chen Lin. With a great sense of relief, Kou Chu unburdened herself to the emperor's faithful eunuch. Chen Lin was shocked beyond words. He took the baby from Kou Chu and paced up and down, racking his brain. Finally he spoke,

'I know what we should do. Let me bring him to Ba Qian Sui, the emperor's eighth brother. The little prince will be safe there.' So saying he placed the baby into one of the boxes used to keep the birthday presents for the eighth prince and slipped away.

In the imperial palace the emperor threw himself into a rage when he saw with his own eyes the monstrous creature which resembled a wild cat. How could his beloved concubine give birth to such a monster?

'I am sure this creature is not fathered by me!' he thundered as he paced up and down. Shaking his head in anger and shame he ordered Li Chen Fei banished to the Palace of Solitude.

Feeling triumphant Liu Fei impatiently awaited the day her own baby would arrive, when she would be made empress. Meanwhile, the emperor drowned his sorrow with wine and more wine, until the day Liu Fei gave birth, to a baby boy. Then the emperor was all smiles again. Banquet after banquet were given; fireworks lit the sky with myriad colours brighter and prettier than the stars; operas were performed night and day. And Liu Fei was crowned empress.

But the empress was not entirely happy. There was a thorn in her side. So long as Li Chen Fei was alive she was afraid that she would be found out one day. Her maid, Kou Chu, had been despatched quite easily with a little poison in her food, so was the midwife. But Li Chen Fei? What to do with her? Again, her uncle was consulted. Guo Huai suggested that they got rid of Li Chen Fei by setting the Palace of Solitude on fire.

However, Li Chen Fei escaped death. One of her loyal attendants made Li Chen Fei exchange clothes with her and bade her run away, disguised as a palace maid, in the chaos that followed the discovery of the fire. The charred body that was found was not Li Chen Fei as the empress thought but that of her faithful maid, Chun Er.

Cast into a world no longer familiar to her, Li Chen Fei eked out a meagre life in a little village, gathering firewood in the forest bordering it. One day, resting on a tree stump, she burst into tears because she was tired, her muscles were aching and there was still the day's meal to be earned. A strapping youth came up to her to ask her why she was crying. When she explained to him why she was in tears, the compassionate young man said,

'Why don't you come home with me? I am an orphan and have always wanted a mother. You can help me keep my little hut clean, cook me my meals and I will look after you as if you are my own mother.'

Gratefully, she accepted the young man's offer. She grew fond of Hai Shou who turned out to be a filial son. However Hai Shou reminded her each day of her own lost son, flesh of her flesh, and she cried herself to sleep every night. Before long she lost her sight.

In the imperial palace the emperor was quite contented now that he had an heir to the throne. But misfortune struck the imperial household once again. The six-year-old crown prince fell from a tree he was climbing and died.

It was at this time that the eighth prince brought his little nephew to see the emperor.

'Your Majesty, this is my son and your very own nephew. If you wish, he can live here with you and be your son.'

The emperor took a good look at the bright-eyed boy and liked him instantly. So he decided to adopt his 'nephew', little knowing that this was indeed his firstborn, the rightful heir to his throne. The empress was in no position to protest as she could not produce another son. So Prince Ren Zhong grew up to become emperor of the Middle Kingdom after all.

• • • • •

It was the custom of Justice Bao to tour the towns and villages from time to time to check on the local magistrates. He often travelled incognito and only revealed his true identity after he was satisfied with what he had learnt, whence he would ostensibly arrive at the town or village in an impressive procession befitting the inspector. In this way, he often would stumble upon an injustice and reopen the case. He was well known for his integrity and when it was heard that he was coming, the people would line the road and await his procession with petitions.

When Li Chen Fei heard that the inspector was visiting her village, she made her son take a petition to him at the village temple where he was stopping. Justice Bao read her case with interest and went personally to her humble hut to see her. Upon seeing the golden ball with her name engraved, Justice Bao realized that she was indeed the empress dowager. He immediately fell to his knees and asked for forgiveness for not recognizing her earlier.

Justice Bao brought Li Chen Fei back to the imperial city first to see the emperor's uncle and then to seek an audience with the emperor. The emperor was enraged when he learnt the truth. Tears of regret for the years of hardship his mother had to bear fell from his eyes as he embraced his now sightless mother.

There was not enough proof to capture the empress dowager and her cunning uncle, Guo Huai. But the resourceful Justice Bao thought of a plan. He invited Guo Huai for a drink and made him terribly drunk. Then he led him to a chamber blazing with fire, where thunder crashed as the cries of

狸貓換太子之包公見李妃

Justice Bao begs forgiveness from Li Chen Fei for not recognizing her earlier.

tortured souls echoed again and again. Guo Huai was told that he was in the first court of hell and there was no way he could cheat the judge of the court of hell. Guo Huai, who truly believed that he was dead, immediately fell to his knees and begged for mercy for his crimes. At this point the crashing thunder and tortured cries stopped, and the fire was doused. He realized too late that this was a ruse to extract his confession.

Guo Huai was executed. His niece, the empress dowager, killed herself when she learnt that the truth was known. Li Chen Fei was reinstated as empress dowager; her adopted son refused a life of luxury in the imperial palace, but accepted a gift of a more solidly built abode. Justice Bao continued to travel the land rooting out corruption and righting wrongs.

Twenty-four Filial Stories

Central to the teachings of Confucius, which influence Chinese thought and behaviour, is filial piety. It is no wonder then that many stories of filial piety (or 'unpiety') abound in Chinese folklore, not a few of them dramatized in operas. The most popular stories have been collected in an anthology known as the Twenty-four Filial Stories. *Of these, the most touching one is the devotion of Wang Chang towards his stepmother who treated him badly.*

Wang Chang's mother died when he was only a child. A few years after his mother's death, his father remarried. His stepmother was a sharp-tongued and harsh woman. She did not hide her contempt and dislike for Wang Chang whom she treated badly whenever his father's back was turned. Wang Chang fetched and carried, chopped the firewood, did the washing, all the housework which the stepmother should be doing but which she loathed. There was one thing she enjoyed though, and that was steamed fresh fish. She loved it so much that she must have steamed fresh fish for all her dinners. And Wang Chang was made responsible for catching the fish for dinner.

One mid-winter morning Wang Chang returned home carrying a pile of wood.

'So you are back. You've been out for nearly an hour. I hope you have not been playing truant, have you? Where is the fish for my dinner?' said Wang Chang's stepmother, her words tumbling out loud and fast as if they were a string of crackers on fire.

'Don't worry, mother. I'll get the fish right away,' Wang Chang said with a cheerful smile even though he had no idea where on earth he could catch a fish when all the ponds and streams nearby were frozen. His face was still numbed by the icy wind which seared it while he was in the forest gathering the firewood.

Wang Chang, clad in a shabby and worn-out jacket, left the house with a fish basket and a fishing rod. He was too preoccupied with the fear of not getting the carp that his stepmother wanted for dinner to feel the cold, cutting wind on his blistered face. He walked swiftly along the banks of the lake, lined with old pine trees which seemed to bend with the cold wind blowing across the lake. The lake was still. Not a ripple could be seen. The entire lake was iced over. Wang Chang surveyed the lake and saw that there was practically no hope of finding a water hole.

Wang Chang felt wretched. He could picture how his stepmother would scream at him and humiliate him if he failed to bring home some fish. He was quite accustomed to such intimidation and humiliation, but he felt duty bound to please his stepmother. Resolutely, Wang Chang walked a few steps over the frozen lake, took off his shabby jacket and laid it on the hard, dry ice. Then, folding his arms around his body, he lowered himself on to the jacket and lay on it, curled up to keep out the cold. He could feel the wind cutting into his back at the same time as it stirred the bare, desolate branches of the trees. Wang Chang pulled himself together tighter to keep

99

To Wang Chang's joy, a fish jumps out of the water-hole.

warm, but to no avail, and he lay half frozen on the lake. Wang Chang tried hard not to focus his mind on his suffering. His entire body was trembling with cold but he kept telling himself,

'Come on, stay calm. Soon the ice will melt and a fish will come. Have faith.'

Wang Chang remained motionless for what seemed to him like an eternity. Then he felt wet. The ice was beginning to melt! He braced himself against the cold wetness which was seeping through his thin clothes and making him tremble more. Slowly, too slowly for him, the ice melted and he could feel the wetness growing into a puddle. He jumped to his feet and used his bare hands to break the now thin layer of ice where he had lain.

As he broke the ice, something jumped out of the water hole. To his indescribable joy, it was a carp. Laughing now, a new warmth flooding his body, he caught hold of the carp, put it into the fish basket and ran all the way home, bare shouldered. The icy cold wind was but a sensation of lightness and freshness to him as he flew through the forest paths and country lanes. When Wang Chang arrived home and presented the fish to his stepmother, even the hardhearted woman was touched. The story was told and retold and soon the whole village heard about the story of Wang Chang and everyone who heard it was deeply touched.

Ji Gong the eccentric but kind-hearted Boddhisattva.

Ji Gong

Ji Gong was a monk, believed to have lived during the Southern Song period (A.D. 1127–1279). He was also known as Da Dian Fo (Eccentric Boddhisattva) because of his fun loving ways: he was often seen eating, drinking and merrymaking. However, his unkempt and careless appearance belied his sharp intelligence and compassion. He used his wushu skills and magical powers to heal the sick and help the poor and needy. Stories of his good deeds have been handed down from generation to generation.

Li Mao Chun was a well-to-do government official of the Song administration. When Li reached middle age he was rather anxious to have a son to carry on the family name and to look after him and his wife in their old age. He and his wife prayed fervently every day for a son.

One warm night his wife had a strange dream. In it she saw a Boddhisattva in long robes and wearing a compassionate smile on his face walking up to her and presenting her with a multi-coloured lotus flower.

'Your prayers will be answered. Take this and eat it,' the Boddhisattva said as he nodded at Mrs Li.

'Thank you,' Mrs Li whispered and she swallowed the lotus

flower. She could feel the flower going through her body and as it reached her stomach she awoke perspiring profusely.

Mrs Li soon found that she was pregnant. Li Mao Chun was overjoyed and took good care of her. Ten months later she gave birth to a lovely baby boy. The baby was named Li Xiu Yuan. He had fine facial features and a healthy complexion. Everyone adored him as he was a beautiful child.

Xiu Yuan grew up in a happy environment and a comfortable home. Both his parents were very fond and proud of him, but they made sure that he was not spoilt by the material things they could offer him. They also encouraged him to study well and understand the Daoist teachings.

Xiu Yuan was an inquisitive student and very interested in Daoist doctrines. When he was barely seven years old he became a disciple of a Daoist monk who taught him *wushu* as well as Daoist philosophy. By fourteen, Xiu Yuan was well versed in poetry, Daoist philosophy, *wushu* and the art of healing.

Then, to Xiu Yuan's sorrow, his father passed away after a serious illness. His mother died two years later. Alone now, he buried himself in the study of Daoist doctrines. Finally he decided to become a monk. So he left home and was ordained a monk at the Ning Ying Temple in Xi Hu. He was given the religious name of Dao Ji.

During the next three years Dao Ji learnt as much as he could from his elders. He became an expert in many fields and was well known for his willingness to help others. But he also became eccentric and withdrawn, often eating and sitting by himself, living in a world of his very own. Even the abbot could not do much to change his ways. He was often found drunk and he was always cheerful and jovial. Thus, people nicknamed him Ji Dian, the helpful and eccentric one. He was also known as Ji Gong, or Ji the Respected, for the people respected him.

One day Ji Gong was taking a stroll just outside the temple

when to his horror he saw a man trying to hang himself. Without delay, Ji Gong thought of a plan to save the poor man. He screamed at the top of his voice,

'I am fed up! I want to die!'

The man, who was just about to place his neck on his sash which was slung over a branch, hesitated when he heard Ji Gong's cry. He walked over to Ji Gong and asked him why he wanted to die. Ji Gong replied that he had no wish to live because he had lost the money from his alms. The man, who was kind hearted, offered Ji Gong everything he had. Ji Gong, however, pretended to be inconsolable. Then he turned around and asked the man why he wanted to kill himself.

The man, whose name was Dong Shi Hong, related that he had sold his daughter to be a maid of a rich merchant because he needed money to pay for his sick mother's medication. He spent the next ten years slaving and saving for his daughter's redemption money. However, to his utter sorrow, when he went to the merchant's house to retrieve his daughter, he found that the family had left the town, and nobody knew where they had moved to. To make things worse, on his way home, he found that his hard-earned money had been stolen. In a moment of dark despair, he saw no reason to live.

At the end of Dong Shi Hong's story Ji Gong looked at him and said quietly, 'I promise you that you will be reunited with your daughter soon.'

Somewhat sceptical, Dong Shi Hong went with Ji Gong to a neighbouring town. When they arrived Ji Gong took him to the street outside a large mansion and asked him to wait there. He also instructed Dong Shi Hong to give his birth date to the person who would come and ask him for it soon. Although perplexed, Dong Shi Hong nodded his head.

Ji Gong then went up the steps leading to the entrance of the mansion and asked the servant standing there if it was true that his master's mother was ill. The servant was quite puzzled by such a question from a complete stranger. He told the strange-looking monk that his master, Yue, had already gone to fetch the best physician in that area to attend to his mother. Ji Gong asserted that no one but he could cure Yue's mother. No sooner had he finished his sentence than Yue appeared with a physician. When the servant told him what the scruffy-looking monk had claimed, the anxious merchant politely said that he had already found a physician and instructed the servant to give the monk some refreshments and alms before sending him on his way. With that, he hurried into the house with the physician.

To Yue's dismay, the physician, upon taking the pulse of the old matriarch, shook his head and said regretfully that there was nothing he could do for her. After the physician had left, Yue sat in the sick room, his head in his hands. Then suddenly his head jerked up as he remembered something. Hurriedly, he went out to the front hall, where Ji Gong was quietly enjoying the chicken and good wine which the disapproving servant had brought him at his request.

Yue was too distraught to notice what he was eating, but asked, 'Venerable One, did you say earlier that you could cure my mother of her illness?'

'Exactly,' Ji Gong paused and smacked his lips.

'Would you like to examine her please?'

'Gladly.'

Within minutes Ji Gong had brought the old lady out of coma and shortly after that she was completely well again. While Yue could not understand how Ji Gong did it, he was grateful to him for giving his mother a new lease of life. He then confessed that his son was also very seriously ill and begged Ji Gong to treat him as well.

Ji Gong took the pulse of the young man and said evenly, 'Although is easy to diagnose your son's illness, it is difficult to cure him. He has to drink the tears of two persons who are born on these dates.' He then gave the birth dates of Dong Shi Hong and his daughter.

Yue immediately sent his men out to the town to search for persons having these birth dates. It was not difficult to find Dong Shi Hong as he was sitting on an upturned bucket outside the house. And Dong Shi Hong's daughter, on hearing what was required to save the young Yue, quickly stepped forward as her young master had been kind to her.

When Dong Shi Hong was brought into the room where the sick young man lay, father and daughter fell into each other's arms and wept with joy. Ji Gong, as usual quick to act, took out a pill from his tattered coat and wet it with tears from Dong Shi Hong and his daughter. He then made young Yue swallow it with a cup of water. Immediately the young man recovered.

At the feast that was immediately laid out to celebrate the double happiness, Ji Gong related to Yue how Dong Shi Hong had saved money with the intention to redeem his daughter from her bond but lost it and tried to end his life. Yue, who was grateful to Dong Shi Hong and his daughter for saving his son's life, immediately tore up the contract and said,

'From today, you are no longer maid of the house of Yue. You can go home to your father.'

So saying, he gave Dong Shi Hong some silver pieces and bade him take good care of his daughter.

Emperor Kang Xi and the vagabond.

Emperor Kang Xi

Emperor Kang Xi, the second emperor of the Qing dynasty (1662–1722), was one of the more illustrious and colourful Qing emperors. Numerous stories have been written about the dynamic emperor who did not believe in half measures. Because he often wore worn-out garments as he disliked extravagance, during his reign old garments became so popular they cost more than new ones! Once he had a dream in which a vagabond told him that he was the emperor's long lost brother, and he spared no effort in tracing the vagabond. When the vagabond was found he was brought to the palace and given a royal treatment. This caused the ire of his wicked ministers who plotted against the vagabond. Kang Xi outwitted his ministers and then had his 'brother' weighed every day to make sure that he was healthy and well.

Another favourite tale about Emperor Kang Xi revolves around his one-hundred-and-eight-course dinner.

Everyday, during the morning, Emperor Kang Xi had an audience with his ministers and other officials to discuss state matters. One day, after the usual round of discussion concerning the political and economic affairs of the country, he asked his prime minister some personal questions regarding his daily expenditure including cost of meals and entertainment. The prime minister informed him that at his old age he ate little and his meal consisted of no more than a bowl of fried bean curd and two meat-filled buns which cost about two small bronze coins. Emperor Kang Xi thought over what his prime minister had said. In his heart he felt that his daily meals were far too rich and sumptuous.

On the following day Emperor Kang Xi summoned his attendants, cooks and housekeepers and told them that from that day onwards he wished to have only a bowl of fried bean curd and two meat-filled buns instead of the usual one hundred and eight courses of delicacies for meals. His subjects were perplexed by what he said but dared not utter a word.

After a period of eating nothing but a bowl of fried bean curd and two meat-filled buns, Emperor Kang Xi summoned his Chief Housekeeper and asked if it was true that each of his meals cost only two bronze coins. To his bewilderment he was told that each of the supposedly simple meals cost a thousand pieces of gold.

'This is preposterous. How is it possible to spend so much on so simple a meal?' asked the emperor.

'Your Majesty, please let me explain. The bean curd for your meal was no ordinary bean curd. It was made from the choicest beans in the entire country. The beans were ground by a grinder specially made from the finest stone which was obtained by cutting deep into the highest hill in the country. The oil for frying was the purest in the land. The buns we served you were chosen from a thousand we made so that they were the very best in terms of shape and fragrance,' the Chief Housekeeper enumerated.

'I don't believe this...'the emperor exclaimed as he paced up and down the hall.

'Your Majesty, may I explain further. The total cost of one meal includes the labour cost of cutting the fragrant wood trees on the hills for firewood, obtaining the stone and shaping it into a fine grinder, and searching for the best oil in the country as well as choosing the best buns...' the Chief Housekeeper added.

'Are you saying that a simple meal of bean curd costs more than a meal of one hundred and eight courses?' asked the emperor in anger.

The Chief Housekeeper promptly threw himself on the floor and asked for forgiveness, saying,

'Your Majesty, you are the son of heaven, you must have everything that is the best in this world. We cannot defy the mandate of the heavens!'

Realizing that he could not save cost by having simple meals Emperor Kang Xi ordered his Chief Housekeeper to have his usual meals served and, if he felt it necessary, let it be one hundred and eight courses so long as such meals would not cost a thousand pieces of gold! The emperor found that he was powerless against tradition although he was the son of heaven.